*a Simple Steps™ Brand Cookbook*

# My MARCATO PASTA MAKER *Homemade* PASTA COOKBOOK

*101 Pastas, Traditional & Modern Recipes, How to Make Pasta by Hand, Artisan Pasta Making Cookbook, from Simple Steps!*

By

Julia Stefano

Simple Steps™ Cookbooks

San Francisco

# *LEGAL NOTICE*

COPYRIGHT © 2019 Simple Steps Cookbooks
First published 2019

All rights reserved. No part of this book may be reproduced in any form or by any electronic or mechanical means, including information storage and retrieval systems, without permission in writing from the publisher, except by reviewers, who may quote brief passages in a review.

Editor: Simple Steps Cookbooks
Art Direction: Simple Steps Cookbooks
Illustrations: Simple Steps Cookbooks
All photographs in this book © Simple Steps Cookbooks or © Depositphotos.com

Published in the United States of America by Simple Steps Cookbooks
www.SimpleStepsCookbooks.com
268 Bush St, #3042
San Francisco, CA 94104 USA

Disclaimer:

Marcato® is a registered trademark of Marcato S.r.l.. This book is independently published by Simple Steps Cookbooks, and it is written to be compatible with the Marcato. This book is not authorized or endorsed by Marcato or its affiliates. Although the publisher and author of this book are practically obsessed with modern cooking techniques, neither represent, nor are associated or affiliated with, any of the brands mentioned in this text.

All content herein represents the author's own experiences and opinions, and do not represent medical or health advice. The responsibility for the consequences of your actions, including your use or misuse of any suggestion or procedure described in this book lies not with the authors, publisher or distributors of this book. We recommend consulting with a licensed health professional before changing your diet or exercise. The author or the publisher does not assume any liability for the use of or inability to use any or all of the information contained in this book, nor does the author or publisher accept responsibility for any type of loss or damage that may be experienced by the user as the result of activities occurring from the use of any information in this book. Use the information responsibly and at your own risk.

The author reserves the right to make changes he or she deems required to future versions of the publication to maintain accuracy.

# *INTRODUCTION*

## *Why You Need This Book*

There are many books out there about pasta making, but this is the only book that will help turn you into a pasta making pro using the Marcato pasta maker. As you may already know, the Marcato pasta maker has been the industry standard for manual pasta makers for many years because of its superior quality, durability, and amazing ease of use. From simple spaghetti to exotic flavored and filled pastas, the Marcato can make many of your favorites as well as pastas you may have seen only at high-end Italian restaurants. And because it is so simple, you will be on your way to making amazing homemade pasta creations in no time. This book will cover everything you need to get the most out of your Marcato pasta maker, including in-depth instructions, recipes, and valuable pro tips on how to make the best pasta you've ever eaten.

## *Unlock Your Marcato's Potential for Amazing Pasta Dishes*

Pasta is perhaps one of the simplest yet most popular foods around the globe, and yet very few people make pasta from scratch. For many years now, most of us have relied on dried store-bought pasta because it is a fast and easy meal. Once you've had real, freshly made pasta you will recognize just how amazing it truly is, and your Marcato pasta maker will put you on the path to making delicious fresh pasta in no time. Because the Marcato is so easy to operate, you can master your favorite types of pasta any time you want. The Marcato is designed to make a variety of different types of pasta, but most importantly, it will allow you to have complete control over the thickness and shape of your pasta. Its easy-to-use controls will have you making perfect pasta instantly - just imagine having delicious, flavorful pasta whenever you want!

## *Amazing Pro Tips for Making the Best Pasta You've Ever Had*

When most of us think about making fresh pasta, we think the same thing: this is going to be difficult, and how do I know it will even come out right? Well, thanks to our valuable pro tips, you will become a pasta professional in no time. We cover everything you need to know, from how to perfect different types of dough, to how to evenly cut your pasta, plus detailed cooking techniques. These industry-tested techniques will show you exactly how to get the very best results from your Marcato pasta maker as soon as you get started. Once you've mastered these techniques, you will never have to settle for dried pasta ever again. In addition to showing you how to make restaurant-quality pasta, we're also going to provide valuable tips on how to make the healthiest pasta you've ever had, while still maintaining amazing flavor and texture.

## *Over 100 Delicious Recipes for Creative Pasta Dishes*

Not only will this book teach you how to use your Marcato pasta maker for perfectly-made pasta, we also include over one hundred recipes for amazing pasta dishes. From different types of pasta dough, to fun shapes and flavorful sauces, this book will give you step-by-step instructions for making the most interesting pasta dishes you've ever had.

## *It's the Only Pasta Recipe Book You'll Ever Need*

The reason why pasta is a staple for cuisines around the world is because it is the perfect canvas for flavor. Many different cultures have their own types of pasta because people all over the world have realized the many benefits of having pasta in their diet. This book includes everything you need, from step-by-step instruction, to recipes and ideas to take your pasta dishes to the next level. You now have all the tools you need to make and cook pasta like the pros, and because the Marcato is so easy to use and maintain, you will find yourself wanting to make pasta all the time.

# CONTENTS

**WHAT CAN YOUR PASTA MAKER DO?** ........................................................................ 8

**HEALTH BENEFITS OF MAKING YOUR OWN PASTA** ............................................... 12

**HISTORY OF PASTA** ...................................................................................................... 15

**HOW TO USE YOUR PASTA MAKER LIKE A PRO** .................................................... 18

**PRO TIPS** ......................................................................................................................... 22

**PANTRY** ........................................................................................................................... 25
- Simple Marinara ........................................................................................................ 28
- Simple Alfredo .......................................................................................................... 29
- Simple Pesto ............................................................................................................. 30

**PASTA DOUGHS** ............................................................................................................. 31
- Classic Egg Pasta Dough ........................................................................................ 32
- Spinach Pasta Dough .............................................................................................. 33
- Sun-Dried Tomato Pasta ......................................................................................... 34
- Buckwheat Pasta Dough ......................................................................................... 35
- Squid Ink Pasta Dough ............................................................................................ 36
- Beet Pasta Dough ..................................................................................................... 37
- Whole Wheat Pasta Dough ..................................................................................... 38
- Rice Noodle Dough .................................................................................................. 39

**VEGETABLE PASTA DISHES** ......................................................................................... 40
- Spaghetti with Fresh Tomato Sauce ..................................................................... 41
- Asparagus Fettuccini Alfredo ................................................................................ 42
- Spinach Lasagna ....................................................................................................... 43
- Basil Fettuccini with a Garlic Lemon Sauce ........................................................ 45
- Sun-Dried Tomato and Mushroom Linguini ........................................................ 46
- White Wine and Zucchini Fettuccini ..................................................................... 48
- Mediterranean Spaghetti ........................................................................................ 49
- Spaghetti Pomodoro ................................................................................................ 50
- Spaghetti alla Puttanesca ....................................................................................... 51
- Linguini with Creamy Butternut Squash Sauce .................................................. 52
- Roasted Cauliflower Spaghetti Marinara ............................................................. 54
- Linguini with Eggplant and Miso Butter .............................................................. 56
- Arugula Walnut Pesto .............................................................................................. 57
- Roasted Red Pepper Fettuccini ............................................................................. 58

**MEAT RECIPES** ............................................................................................................... 59
- Classic Bolognese ..................................................................................................... 60
- Spaghetti alla Carbonara ........................................................................................ 62

    Pasta with Ricotta Meatballs ............................................................................. 63
    Chicken Piccata with Capellini .......................................................................... 65
    One Pot Chicken Pasta ..................................................................................... 67
    Ham and Leek Pasta ......................................................................................... 68
    Pepper Steak Pasta ........................................................................................... 69
    Spaghetti with Sausage and Tomatoes ............................................................. 70
    Classic Beef Stroganoff ..................................................................................... 71
    Spicy Lamb and Fennel Fettuccini .................................................................... 73
    Linguini with Chicken and Prosciutto ................................................................ 74
    Spaghetti with Sausage and Radicchio ............................................................. 75
    Grandma's Spaghetti with Red Sauce and Meatballs ....................................... 76
    Tagliatelle with Heart Vodka Sauce .................................................................. 78
    Fettuccini with Pancetta Cream Sauce ............................................................. 79
    Chicken Milano ................................................................................................. 81
    Cajun Steak Spaghetti ...................................................................................... 82
    Delicata Squash Carbonara .............................................................................. 84
    Eggplant and Prosciutto Ragu .......................................................................... 85
    Beef Short Rib Ragu ......................................................................................... 86

**SEAFOOD DISHES** ................................................................................................ **88**
    Linguini with White Clam Sauce ....................................................................... 89
    Spaghetti with Shrimp and Tomato Sauce ....................................................... 91
    Smoked Salmon Alfredo ................................................................................... 92
    Linguini al Frutti di Mare ................................................................................... 93
    Shrimp Scampi ................................................................................................. 94
    Pappardelle with Salmon and Peas in Pesto Cream ........................................ 95
    Lobster and Gruyere Fettuccini ........................................................................ 96
    Shrimp and Brie Linguini .................................................................................. 97
    Capellini with Bay Scallops ............................................................................... 98
    Spaghetti with Spicy Mussels ........................................................................... 99
    Linguini with Calamari and Fennel ................................................................. 100
    Spicy Tilapia Spaghetti ................................................................................... 101
    Linguini with Red Clam Sauce ....................................................................... 103
    Fideua ............................................................................................................. 104
    Seafood Arrabbiata ......................................................................................... 106
    Shrimp Carbonara ........................................................................................... 108
    Spaghetti with Salmon and Leeks .................................................................. 109
    Fettuccini with Crab, Cherry Tomatoes, and Basil .......................................... 110
    Creamy Lobster Linguini ................................................................................. 111
    Capellini with Oysters ..................................................................................... 112

**FILLED PASTA DISHES** ..................................................................................... **113**
    Ricotta Ravioli ................................................................................................. 114
    Ravioli with Sage Walnut Butter ..................................................................... 115
    Crab Ravioli with Tomato Cream .................................................................... 116
    Fig and Gorgonzola Ravioli ............................................................................. 117
    Three Cheese Tortellini ................................................................................... 118
    Beef and Pork Filled Tortellini ......................................................................... 119

| | |
|---|---|
| MUSHROOM TORTELLINI | 120 |
| BUTTERNUT SQUASH RAVIOLI | 122 |
| SAUSAGE RAVIOLI | 123 |
| CHICKEN AND SPINACH RAVIOLI | 124 |
| BOLOGNESE RAVIOLI WITH FRESH TOMATO SAUCE | 125 |
| CREAMY FOUR-CHEESE RAVIOLI | 127 |
| PUMPKIN RAVIOLI | 128 |

**BAKED PASTAS** ............................................................................................**129**

| | |
|---|---|
| BAKED FOUR-CHEESE SPAGHETTI | 130 |
| CLASSIC MEAT LASAGNA | 131 |
| ROASTED BUTTERNUT SQUASH LASAGNA | 133 |
| BAKED MANICOTTI | 135 |
| BAKED SPAGHETTI MARINARA | 136 |
| ROASTED VEGETABLE AND RAVIOLI LASAGNA | 138 |
| PUMPKIN LASAGNA | 139 |
| BAKED TAGLIATELLE WITH CHICKEN | 140 |
| FETTUCCINI AL FORNO | 141 |
| BAKED PASTA PRIMAVERA | 142 |
| CHEESY BAKED TORTELLINI | 144 |
| BAKED CHICKEN CANNELLONI | 145 |

**ASIAN PASTA DISHES** ....................................................................................**146**

| | |
|---|---|
| CHICKEN CHOW MEIN | 147 |
| CLASSIC PAD THAI | 148 |
| SPICY COLD PEANUT NOODLES | 149 |
| BEEF NOODLE STIR FRY | 150 |
| SESAME NOODLES | 152 |
| PAD SEE EW | 153 |
| SHRIMP LO MEIN | 154 |
| MISO NOODLES | 155 |
| SHIITAKE AND SCALLION NOODLES | 156 |
| RAMEN SALAD WITH PEANUTS | 157 |
| RED CURRY NOODLES | 158 |
| PANCIT | 159 |
| SHANGHAI NOODLES | 160 |
| TAIWANESE BEEF NOODLE SOUP | 161 |

# 1

---

## WHAT CAN YOUR PASTA MAKER DO?

## *You Can Make a Variety of Different Types of Pasta*

One of the most attractive aspects of your Marcato pasta maker is its versatility. With Marcato's wide range of cutting attachments, you will be able to make virtually any type of pasta. The Marcato comes equipped with a cutting attachment that allows you to make traditional-size spaghetti, as well as fettuccini and wide pasta sheets. With plain pasta sheets you can make delicious noodles for lasagna, as well as filled pastas like ravioli, tortellini, and cannelloni. You can add attachments that will also allow you to make capellini, linguini, ravioli, and tagliatelle. With this many options, you will be able to make a wide variety of different pastas with your Marcato pasta maker, and all of them will be precisely cut.

## *Easily Control the Thickness of Your Pasta*

Different pastas are best at different thicknesses, and thanks to the Marcato's thickness knob, you are able to control for the exact thickness as you roll out your pasta dough. By incrementally reducing the thickness of the dough you are also performing another important pasta making function: properly conditioning the dough. When the dough is ready to be rolled it may still have a bit of roughness to it. By gradually pressing the dough thinner and thinner, you will create a smoother texture resulting in perfect pasta. To change the thickness of the dough, all you need to do is start at zero and run the dough through several times; then increase the numbers, passing the dough through each time until you have reached your desired thickness. Once you have done this, you can either use the sheets or run them through a cutting attachment.

## *Cut Pasta Into Your Favorite Styles*

Some pasta makers only allow you to make one type of pasta, but the Marcato pasta maker is so versatile that it will allow you to create almost any type of pasta quickly and easily. The most common types of pasta are spaghetti, linguini, and fettuccini, and the Marcato easily makes these styles with a simple cutting attachment. However, you can also make more exotic styles like tagliatelle and perfectly uniform ravioli by using additional attachments that are available for your Marcato pasta maker. Many people are also now discovering delicious hand-formed pastas such as orecchiette, farfalle, and cavatelli. Using the Marcato's easy thickness control, you will be able to craft these pastas by first rolling out dough with the perfect thickness.

## *You Can Make Amazing Filled Pastas*

Who doesn't love perfectly filled ravioli, tortellini, and cannelloni? Thanks to your Marcato pasta maker you can make all of these filled pastas in a variety of different ways. For ravioli, you can purchase a cutting attachment that will roll out perfectly uniform raviolis, but you can also make more rustic filled pastas by creating perfect pasta sheets with your Marcato and filling them however you desire. This way, if you want to make jumbo lobster raviolis, you can customize them to your taste.

## *Make Perfect Crackers and Flatbreads*

The Marcato pasta maker is designed to make the world's best homemade pasta, but that's not all it can do. One of the main challenges of making perfect crackers and flatbreads is getting them to a uniform thickness. Thanks to the Marcato pasta maker you can ensure that your cracker or flatbread dough is always perfectly uniform and the perfect thickness. Simply run your cracker or flatbread dough through the Marcato the same way you would with pasta. You can experiment with different thicknesses before you cut the dough into shapes.

# 2

## HEALTH BENEFITS OF MAKING YOUR OWN PASTA

## *Get More Protein In Your Pasta By Using Eggs*

We tend to think of pasta as just carbs, and while this is true of store-bought pasta, homemade pasta has a distinct health advantage: more protein. Most homemade pasta contains eggs, which pack a punch of protein and nutrition that would normally be lacking in pasta. You can experiment with different combinations of egg yolks and whites to get just the right flavor and texture. The egg yolks are also the reason why homemade pasta has its unmistakable yellow color that makes every plate feel like a vacation to Italy.

## **Add Vegetables to Your Pasta Dough**

In addition to using eggs for more flavor and nutrition, you can add vegetables for extra nutrients and festive colors that will make your dishes really come alive. By processing vegetables like tomatoes and spinach into a fine paste, you can add these ingredients to your dough for colorful and healthy pasta that has a delightful hint of extra flavor in every bite. Once you have tried experimenting with simple things like spinach and tomatoes, you can try using things like sundried tomatoes and peppers to further spice up your pasta.

## *Make Healthy Whole Wheat Pasta*

Another way to add extra flavor and nutrition to your pasta is by making it with whole wheat flour. Whole wheat flour is a great source of vitamins, minerals, and fiber. It is lower in simple carbohydrates, so it is a great choice for people who are still looking to enjoy delicious pasta dishes but are trying to cut out some of the unnecessary sugar found in typical white flours. And because you can control the amount of whole wheat flour to white flour, you can customize your pasta dough for the exact flavor you desire.

## *Make Gluten-Free Noodles*

It's easy to forget that pasta isn't just Italian. Many cultures around the world have been enjoying some variety of pasta for thousands of years because it is a simple staple that is tasty, filling, and easy to make. Many cuisines make noodles out of flours other than wheat flour. For instance, many Asian cuisines feature rice noodles that are a great choice for stir fry and soups. These types of noodles are also great for those looking for gluten-free options, because rice flour, unlike wheat flour, contains no gluten.

## *Use the Freshest Ingredients to Make the Healthiest Pasta*

One of the best aspects of making your own pasta with the Marcato pasta maker is the ability to control exactly what ingredients you are using. Unlike with store bought pasta, you can make your pasta with the freshest, high-quality eggs and the best flour for the tastiest results. In the recipes section we will go into depth about how to make the most delicious pasta you've ever had, and fun ways to make sauces and toppings that will take your dishes to the next level.

# 3

---

## HISTORY OF PASTA

## *Where Did Pasta Originate?*

While there are many stories about where pasta came from, most historians now agree that what we think of as pasta originated in the Roman Empire around two thousand years ago. There is also evidence that pasta was developed in Greece and North Africa at around this same time. It is then believed that pasta-making quickly spread, as it was easily dried and transported without refrigeration. Asian countries adopted their own methods of making noodles at an earlier time, but since wheat was not a staple grain in most Asian countries, their noodles tended to be made from rice and other grains. When traders began importing wheat to Asia in larger quantities, they too began making many of their noodles from wheat.

## *How Pasta Became a Staple of the Mediterranean Diet*

Pasta has been a staple food of the Mediterranean region since around the Ninth Century A.D. It was originally adopted because it was easy to make and stable enough to be dried and stored, and it was an important source of nutrition. Pasta is also an excellent vehicle for sauces that highlight Mediterranean flavors like tomatoes and olives. As pasta rose in popularity around the region, it became an important part of the culture, to the point where the Italian government imposed regulations concerning the proper ingredients and methods for preparing fresh pasta.

## *How Different Types of Pasta Came to Exist*

The best explanation for the variety of different shapes of pasta is that each shape is an ideal vehicle for different toppings. The original forms of pasta were mostly thin-cut varieties such as capellini (angel hair) and spaghetti. As time went on, pasta makers realized that cutting pasta into ribbon shapes (like fettuccini and linguini) created a better way to capture certain sauces. Later, extruded pastas like ziti and rigatoni became popular because they were an excellent base for baked recipes. Today chefs are again experimenting with hand-formed pastas, like cavatelli, because of their interesting textures.

## *A Brief Guide to Pastas of the World*

While we most commonly attribute pasta to Italy, there are other types of noodles that have become staples of different cultures. Rice noodles exist in most Asian countries and are the base for soups and stir fry. The Japanese developed udon noodles using imported wheat, and these noodles have been an important part of their cuisine ever since. While we don't generally think of noodle dishes being a big part of Middle Eastern cuisine, pasta traveled from the north of Africa to many parts of the Middle East and they often use wheat noodles for baked and fried dishes.

# 4

# HOW TO USE YOUR PASTA MAKER LIKE A PRO

## *How to Set Up Your Marcato Pasta Maker*

One of the great aspects of your Marcato pasta maker is how easy it is to set up and use. Right out of the box, your Marcato is nearly completely assembled and ready to use. In the box you will find the pasta roller base, the cutting attachment, a stabilizing clamp, and the hand crank. To set up your Marcato, find a hard, flat surface that has a lip. A countertop or table will work best. You will notice a hole on the side of the Marcato near the bottom. Insert the top of the clamp into the hole and turn the clamp screw to affix it firmly to the counter or table. It is important that the Marcato is completely stable or it will be difficult to use. Once it is firmly attached, insert the hand crank into the hole on the upper part of the Marcato base. You are now ready to roll pasta.

## *How to Make Perfect Pasta Dough*

Making fresh pasta dough takes some practice, but after a short time you should be able to quickly recognize the hallmarks of perfect pasta dough. You will want to start with two cups of flour. You can use all-purpose flour, or you can experiment with adding durum or semolina flour to achieve different textures. Make a well in the pile of flour and add two whole eggs and two additional egg yolks. Keep the unused egg whites in case you need to add some extra moisture to your dough. Since eggs vary in size, you may need more or less moisture, but this can easily be adjusted. Add one teaspoon of salt to the mixture before stirring. If you prefer a smoother pasta you can add one tablespoon of olive oil, but if you prefer a more textured pasta you can leave it out. Use a fork to gradually combine the ingredients. At first it will appear too dry, but do not add any liquid to the mixture until you have been stirring for a while. Gradually form the mixture into a ball and knead it until it holds together. Knead the dough, turning it 45 degrees each time, until the dough becomes elastic.

## *How to Roll Out Perfect Dough Every Time*

Once your dough has rested, use a bench knife or other large knife to cut it into quarters. Gently roll each quarter into an oblong ball and flatten slightly. Set the thickness wheel on your Marcato to zero (the widest setting) and feed the dough into the machine by turning the hand crank. After it has been through the machine, fold it over and repeat three times. Once you have done this, you can start changing the thickness one number at a time and running the pasta through the machine. Do not skip thickness settings.

## *How to Use the Cutting Attachment*

Once you have pasta sheets that are the desired thickness, you can use the cutting attachment to cut your pasta into perfectly uniform pieces. The attachment that comes with your Marcato pasta maker will allow you to make spaghetti and fettuccini. Slide the cutting attachment into the guide slots on the side of the base and make sure it is firmly in place. Remove the hand crank from the base and insert it into the side of the cutting attachment. Slowly feed your pasta sheets into the cutter and turn the crank. The sheets will be pulled into the cutter and cut pasta will come out the other side.

## *How to Store Unused Pasta*

In order to store fresh pasta for later use, you will want to dry it in a manner that will avoid the pieces sticking together. The easiest way to do this is to purchase a pasta drying rack. It will allow you to hang pasta so that it can dry and then be stored. Otherwise, you can dry pasta by twisting it into loose piles, but if you do this, be sure to coat it liberally with flour to avoid sticking.

## *How to Properly Clean and Store Your Pasta Maker*

Cleaning the Marcato is perhaps the easiest aspect of using it. Never use water, and never put it in the dishwasher. Once you are finished making pasta, simply run a piece of parchment paper through the rollers like you are rolling out pasta. Repeat this several times and then disassemble the machine. Once disassembled it should fit back into its box for easy storage.

# 5

## PRO TIPS

## *Using Olive Oil to Improve the Texture of Your Dough*

If you've made a few batches of dough and you find that the texture is a bit coarse, you can try using olive oil to make your dough smoother in texture. There are many schools of thought on how to get the best texture from your pasta, but we have found that a tablespoon of olive oil will break down some of the grit in the flour and result in a more refined pasta. Adding a bit of salt can also be helpful in creating a smooth dough.

## *How to Control the Moisture Level of Your Dough*

One of the biggest challenges of pasta dough-making is controlling the moisture level. Since almost all of the moisture is coming from eggs, it can be difficult to get the level just right because eggs vary greatly in size. If your dough simply won't hold together, try rubbing a very small amount of the reserved egg white into the dough. If you end up with sticky dough, try adding just a bit of flour and continue to knead until the dough appears smooth but not sticky.

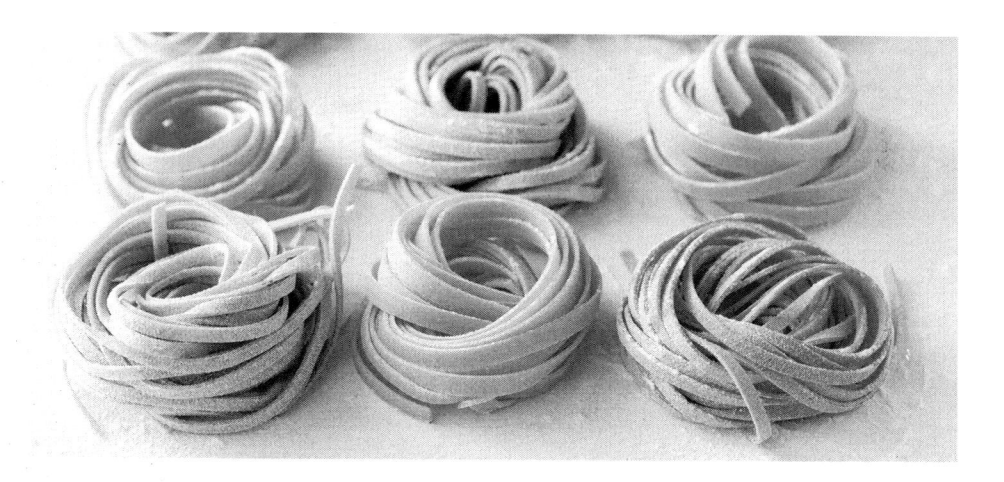

## *Add Flavors to Your Pasta Dough*

There are many ways you can flavor to pasta dough, and you will want to incorporate these flavors into the dough when you make it. The most common flavors to add to your dough are spinach and tomato. These will also color your dough. In order to add these types of flavors to your dough, you will need to thoroughly process either spinach or tomatoes in a food processor. Then, when you are mixing the flour and eggs, add several tablespoons of spinach or tomato to the dough and continue to knead.

## *How to Choose the Perfect Thickness Setting for Your Pasta*

The thickness of pasta is partially a matter of personal taste. Some people prefer theirs a bit thicker or thinner, but in general there is a particular thickness for each type of pasta. You will need to keep in mind that fresh pasta expands even more than dry pasta when it cooks, so dough that appears just right when you cut it may end up too thick after cooking. Your Marcato pasta maker comes with a helpful guide for which thickness level you should be using for each type of pasta you make. Of course, these are only guidelines and you should feel free to try different thickness levels in order to decide what you prefer.

## *The Best Way to Cook Pasta*

To cook your fresh pasta, the best way is to use a large pot. This will allow the pasta to cook without sticking together. Fresh pasta is even more likely to stick together than dry pasta, so having enough room in the pot will be important. You also need to keep in mind that fresh pasta cooks much faster than dry pasta. While it may take 8 to 10 minutes to cook a pot of dry spaghetti, fresh spaghetti will cook in about half that time.

# 6

# **PANTRY**

## *The Best Flours for Perfect Pasta*

While there are many different types of flour available, you may find that you get the best results using all-purpose flour when you begin making your own pasta. It is easy to work with and consistently produces excellent results. As you become a more confident pasta maker, you may want to experiment with semolina flour, which is slightly coarser but does have a richer flavor than all-purpose flour. Most cooks who use semolina do not use only semolina, however. You can experiment to find your favorite ratio, but many pasta makers prefer a mixture of 50% semolina to 50% all-purpose flour for the perfect balance of flavor and texture. In addition to semolina, you can also try substituting some whole wheat flour to your pasta for added nutrition. Since whole wheat flour is also coarser than all-purpose flour, you will most likely want to start with only a small percentage of whole wheat flour and then gradually add more until you find the level that works best for you.

## *Ingredients for Delicious Pasta Fillings*

As we have covered in numerous recipes, there are certain filling ingredients that you will want to keep on hand for your pasta making adventures. Ricotta cheese is a perfect filling for any filled pasta and can also add delightful flavor and texture to other pasta dishes as well. If you are looking for a meatier filling for your pasta, sausage is a perfect filling because, in addition to being delicious, it is very easy to work with. Whether you choose to use traditional Italian hot or sweet sausage, or other sausages such as bratwurst or knockwurst, you are sure to create a pasta that will impress. If you are looking to stay on the vegetarian side, mushrooms make an excellent filling because they impart lots of earthy flavor and will hold together easily for perfectly formed pastas.

## *Fun Ways to Make Easy and Delicious Sauces*

If you are a beginner pasta maker, there are a few simple sauces that you absolutely must know. While this book covers many interesting and exotic sauce recipes, it's always good to have a few sauces that you can throw together at the last minute. Here are three recipes that you really can't live without:

# Simple Marinara

## Ingredients:

*1 28-ounce can crush tomatoes, preferably San Marzano tomatoes*

*3 cloves garlic, minced*

*1 medium onion, minced*

*1 tablespoon fresh oregano, chopped*

*1 tablespoon fresh basil, chopped*

*2 tablespoons olive oil*

*Salt and black pepper*

## Directions:

1. In a saucepan, heat the oil over medium heat and add the garlic and onion. Sauté until soft, then add the rest of the ingredients. Simmer for 30 minutes.

# Simple Alfredo

## Ingredients:

*1/2 cup butter*

*8 ounces cream cheese*

*2 teaspoons garlic powder*

*2 cups milk*

*6 ounces parmesan cheese, grated*

*Salt and black pepper*

## Directions:

1. In a medium saucepan, melt the butter and add the cream cheese and garlic. Stir in the milk slowly and then add the parmesan. Season to taste with salt and pepper.

# Simple Pesto

## Ingredients:

*1 cup fresh basil leaves*

*3 cloves garlic*

*3 tablespoons pine nuts*

*1/3 cup parmesan*

*1/3 cup olive oil*

*Salt and black pepper*

## Directions:

1. In a food processor, combine the basil, garlic, pine nuts, and parmesan. Season with salt and pepper then blend, adding the oil slowly.

## *Delicious Toppings and Garnishes*

The final step in any pasta dish is adding fun and delicious garnishes that complete the meal. While you can experiment with a wide range of garnishes and toppings, there are certain things that go well with almost any pasta and will create a beautifully composed dish. Parmesan cheese is a perfect topping for almost any pasta, but for best results, we recommend grating your own. Pre-grated parmesan is almost always packaged with cellulose to keep it from clumping. Cellulose is actually made from tree bark, and while it does a good job of keeping cheese from sticking together, it also dilutes the flavor of the cheese and changes the texture. We also recommend grating your own mozzarella because pre-grated mozzarella also contains cellulose and as a result, it won't melt as well.

For garnishes, you will want to keep some fresh herbs on hand, as these add just a little extra kick of flavor and a nice hint of color to your dish. Parsley is a great choice because of its subtle earthy flavor, but you can also try experimenting with chopped basil, oregano and sage for different flavors. The great thing is that these garnishes will work well with almost any pasta dish you create, ensuring that your experience making pasta with your Marcato pasta maker is the beginning of a beautiful friendship.

# 7

## PASTA DOUGHS

# Classic Egg Pasta Dough

*The Italians have been making pasta with this dough for centuries, and for good reason. It is simple yet elegant and tasty. Making pasta with this dough is like stepping into your favorite Italian bistro.*

*Servings: 8*
*Prep time: 15 minutes*
*Cook time: 30 minutes*

## Ingredients:

- 2 cups all-purpose flour
- 2 whole eggs
- 2 egg yolks (since eggs vary in size you may need to use additional egg whites)
- 1 teaspoon salt
- 1 tablespoon extra-virgin olive oil

## Directions:

1. On a flat surface, or in a very large bowl, make a mound with the flour. Create a well in the middle of the pile of flour.
2. Add 2 whole eggs and 2 egg yolks to the well in the flour. Then add the salt and olive oil.
3. Using a fork, begin to mix the ingredients. At first it will be very rough and won't hold together, but keep mixing.
4. Once all of the flour has been mixed with the eggs, use a bench knife to scrape it into a rough ball. Use your hands to knead the dough ball against a flat surface. Turn the ball 45 degrees and press the heel of your hand into it.
5. If your dough remains flaky and won't hold together, add just a tiny bit of the reserved egg yolk. If it is too tacky, roll the dough in a very small amount of flour and keep kneading. Once the ball is smooth and elastic, wrap it in plastic wrap and rest it on the counter for 30 minutes. You now have dough that is ready to be rolled into pasta with your Marcato Pasta Maker.

*Nutritional Info: Calories: 158, Sodium: 309 mg, Dietary Fiber: 0.8 g, Total Fat: 4.3 g, Total Carbs: 24.1 g, Protein: 5.3 g.*

# *Spinach Pasta Dough*

*This fun twist on classic pasta dough is an attractive and tasty way to incorporate spinach into your pasta. It can be used to make all of your favorite pasta styles.*

*Servings: 8*
*Prep time: 15 minutes*
*Cook time: 30 minutes*

## Ingredients:

- 6 ounces fresh spinach
- 2 whole eggs
- 1 egg yolk
- 2 1/2 cups all-purpose flour
- 1 tablespoon salt

## Directions:

1. Use a steamer to steam the spinach until it has thoroughly wilted. Then place it in a food processor or blender and blend until smooth. Allow to cool and strain well.

2. In a food processor, combine the eggs and process until smooth, then add the flour, salt, and spinach. Pulse until the dough just starts to come together into a ball.

3. Remove the dough from the food processor and place on a floured surface. Knead with your hands, turning the dough 45 degrees each time, until the dough becomes smooth and elastic. Wrap it in plastic wrap and rest for 30 minutes before using.

4. When you are ready to make pasta, cut the dough into quarters and feed into your Marcato Pasta Maker.

*Nutritional Info: Calories: 170, Sodium: 906 mg, Dietary Fiber: 1.5 g, Total Fat: 2.1 g, Total Carbs: 30.7 g, Protein: 6.4 g.*

# Sun-Dried Tomato Pasta

*Sun-dried tomatoes are an excellent way to add a deep, earthy flavor to your pasta dough, and it also gives your pasta a festive color that is sure to delight.*

*Servings: 8*
*Prep time: 10 minutes*
*Cook time: 30 minutes*

## Ingredients:

*3 eggs*

*2 1/2 cups flour*

*1/3 cup sun-dried tomatoes in olive oil*

*1 teaspoon salt*

## Directions:

1. In a food processor, blend the tomatoes and olive oil until they are a smooth paste.
2. On a large workspace, make a pile with the flour and make a well in the middle. Add the eggs and tomato puree and begin to slowly mix the flour into the eggs.
3. Once the dough starts to come together, form it into a ball and knead with the heel of your hand until the dough becomes elastic. Dust the ball with flour and wrap in plastic wrap and let rest for 30 minutes before cutting.

*Nutritional Info: Calories: 172, Sodium: 362 mg, Dietary Fiber: 1.3 g, Total Fat: 2.1 g, Total Carbs: 31.2 g, Protein: 6.4 g.*

# Buckwheat Pasta Dough

*This healthy alternative to traditional pasta dough is not only healthy, but also has an earthy, rich flavor that is perfect for wide flat pastas like fettuccini or pappardelle.*

*Servings: 8*
*Prep time: 15 minutes*
*Cook time: 30 minutes*

## Ingredients:

- 3 cups all-purpose flour
- 1/2 cup buckwheat flour
- 4 large eggs
- 1 tablespoon olive oil
- 1 teaspoon salt

## Directions:

1. In a mixer using the dough hook, combine the flours, eggs, oil, and salt and mix until a dough begins to form. If the dough is crumbly, add a small amount of water, and if the dough is sticky add a small amount of all-purpose flour.

2. Transfer the dough to a floured workspace and knead until the dough becomes elastic. This usually takes 5 to 10 minutes. Wrap the dough in plastic wrap and allow to rest at room temperature for 30 minutes.

3. Use your Marcato pasta maker to roll out the dough. This type of pasta takes slightly longer to cook than traditional pasta dough.

*Nutritional Info: Calories: 247, Sodium: 327 mg, Dietary Fiber: 2 g, Total Fat: 4.9 g, Total Carbs: 41.3 g, Protein: 8.9 g.*

# Squid Ink Pasta Dough

*This is a simple way to make exotic, rich, flavored pasta dough that is typically cut into either linguini or fettuccini and paired with a hearty tomato-based sauce and fresh seafood.*

*Servings: 6*
*Prep time: 10 minutes*
*Cook time: 30 minutes*

## Ingredients:

- *2 cups all-purpose flour*
- *2 whole eggs*
- *4 egg yolks*
- *4 egg whites*
- *4 teaspoons squid ink*
- *1 teaspoon salt*

## Directions:

1. On a large workspace make a mound with the flour and make a well in the middle. Add the eggs, additional yolks, squid ink, and salt.

2. Use a fork to mix the ingredients until most of the flour has been incorporated. Use a bench knife to scrape the dough off the workspace and form into a rough ball.

3. Flour the workspace and knead the dough until it becomes smooth. Add additional egg white if the dough remains flaky.

4. Once the dough is smooth and elastic, wrap it in plastic wrap and let rest on the counter for 30 minutes before rolling with your Marcato pasta maker.

*Nutritional Info: Calories: 221, Sodium: 453 mg, Dietary Fiber: 1.1 g, Total Fat: 4.9 g, Total Carbs: 32.6 g, Protein: 10.5 g.*

# Beet Pasta Dough

*This vibrant, pink pasta has a mild flavor but a very festive look. Perfect for pasta dishes with lots of colorful vegetables, this bright pasta dough is sure to be a welcome surprise.*

*Servings: 6*
*Prep time: 45 minutes*
*Cook time: 45 minutes*

## Ingredients:

- 2 small beets, peeled
- 2 cups all-purpose flour
- 1 whole egg
- 5 egg yolks
- 1 teaspoon salt

## Directions:

1. Bring a large pot of water to a boil and add the beets. Allow the beets to simmer for 40 to 45 minutes and then remove from the water. Cut the beets into chunks or slices and puree in a food processor until completely smooth.

2. On a large workspace make a mound with the flour and make a well in the middle. Add the egg and yolks as well as the salt and 4 tablespoons of the beet puree.

3. Use a fork to combine the mixture until a rough dough had formed. Then use a bench knife to scrape the dough into a ball.

4. Knead the dough until it becomes smooth and elastic. This will take about 5 to 10 minutes. Then wrap the dough in plastic wrap and allow to rest for 30 to 45 minutes. Your dough will then be ready to cut.

*Nutritional Info: Calories: 214, Sodium: 418 mg, Dietary Fiber: 1.5 g, Total Fat: 4.9 g, Total Carbs: 34 g, Protein: 7.8 g.*

# Whole Wheat Pasta Dough

*For those looking to cut down on white flour, this whole wheat dough is healthier and still extremely flavorful. It has an excellent rustic texture that is perfect for thick hearty sauces.*

*Servings: 8*
*Prep time: 20 minutes*
*Cook time: 30 minutes*

## Ingredients:

- 1 1/2 cups all-purpose flour
- 1 1/2 cups whole wheat flour
- 1/2 teaspoon salt
- 4 whole eggs
- 2 teaspoons olive oil

## Directions:

1. In a mixer, use the dough attachment to slowly combine all ingredients. You can also do this by hand by mixing all of the ingredients in a large bowl with a fork.

2. When all of the ingredients are combined, you should have a rough, sticky dough. Remove it from the bowl and place it on a floured workspace.

3. Knead the dough until it becomes smooth and elastic. Then wrap in plastic wrap and rest for 30 minutes.

*Nutritional Info: Calories: 203, Sodium: 180 mg, Dietary Fiber: 3.4 g, Total Fat: 4 g, Total Carbs: 34.4 g, Protein: 8.3 g.*

# Rice Noodle Dough

*Rice noodles are a staple of many Asian cuisines, and this easy-to-make noodle dough is perfect for making noodles for soups and stir fry, or just eating with simple chili oil. They are also a great gluten-free option.*

*Servings: 4*
*Prep time: 15 minutes*
*Cook time: 30 minutes*

## Ingredients:

*1 1/4 cup rice flour*

*2 tablespoons tapioca starch*

*1/2 teaspoon salt*

*1 1/4 cups water*

*1 teaspoon vegetable oil*

## Directions:

1. In a large bowl, combine the rice flour, tapioca starch, salt, and water. Mix until everything is dissolved and smooth.

2. Add 1 teaspoon of oil and then strain the liquid through a fine mesh strainer. Cover the liquid and rest for 30 minutes

3. Bring a large pot of water to a boil and float a flat pan on the water.

4. Brush a light coating of vegetable oil on the flat pan and coat with the rice noodle mixture. Make sure the rice noodle mixture coats the whole pan evenly. Cover the pot and cook for 5 minutes. Remove the flat pan from the pot and with a spatula slide the sheet of rice noodles onto a cutting board. Allow the noodle sheets to cool and then cut using the fettuccini setting on your Marcato pasta maker.

*Nutritional Info: Calories: 208, Sodium: 293 mg, Dietary Fiber: 1.2 g, Total Fat: 1.8 g, Total Carbs: 43.8 g, Protein: 3 g.*

# 8

## VEGETABLE PASTA DISHES

# Spaghetti with Fresh Tomato Sauce

*This fresh simple dish uses flavorful, fresh tomatoes combined with freshly-made spaghetti for a perfect, light dish that pairs well with a glass of crisp white wine.*

*Servings: 8*
*Prep time: 30 minutes*
*Cook time: 30 minutes*

## Ingredients:

*1 ball of egg pasta dough*

*8 Roma tomatoes, diced*

*1/2 cup Italian dressing*

*1/4 cup basil, chopped*

*2 cloves garlic, finely chopped*

*3 tablespoons olive oil*

*Grated parmesan cheese for topping*

## Directions:

1. Cut one ball of egg pasta dough into quarters, and flatten each quarter slightly. Set your Marcato pasta maker to zero and slowly feed the dough into the machine. Fold the dough and send it through the machine several times and then start rolling the dough thinner one setting at a time.

2. For spaghetti, you will stop rolling the dough after you finish the fifth thickness setting. Attach the cutting attachment and feed the pasta sheets into the side for spaghetti.

3. Boil a large pot of water.

4. Place the cut pasta in loose coils and sprinkle with flour.

5. In a medium saucepan over medium heat, heat the oil and add the garlic and tomatoes. Cook until the tomatoes have softened but are not mushy.

6. Add the pasta to the boiling water and cook the pasta for 2 to 3 minutes. Strain the pasta and toss it into the pan with the tomatoes. Coat the pasta with sauce and add the Italian dressing. Remove from heat, top with the parmesan and basil, and serve.

*Nutritional Info: Calories: 134, Sodium: 51mg, Dietary Fiber: 1.6 g, Total Fat: 10.4 g, Total Carbs: 9.8 g, Protein: 2 g.*

# Asparagus Fettuccini Alfredo

*This fresh take on a classic Alfredo adds flavor as well as texture. The flavorful fettuccini will shine through this light cream sauce.*

*Servings: 8*
*Prep time: 30 minutes*
*Cook time: 20 minutes*

## Ingredients:

1 ball fresh egg pasta dough

1 pound asparagus, chopped

1 cup butter

3/4 pint heavy cream

1 clove garlic, smashed

3/4 cup Romano cheese, grated

1/2 cup parmesan cheese, grated

## Directions:

1. Bring a large pot of water to a boil.
2. Roll out pasta sheets using the Marcato pasta maker to setting #5 and then feed the sheets into the cutting attachment on the fettuccini side.
3. n a large saucepan, melt the butter and add the cream over low heat. Add the garlic and stir for several minutes. Add the cheese and allow to thicken.
4. Chop the asparagus and blanch in the boiling water for 2 minutes. Remove and run under cold water.
5. Add the pasta to the boiling water and cook 2 to 3 minutes. Strain the pasta and add to the sauce. Then add the asparagus and stir well. Serve topped with parmesan cheese.

*Nutritional Info: Calories: 518, Sodium: 592mg, Dietary Fiber: 1.3 g, Total Fat: 49 g, Total Carbs: 8.1 g, Protein: 14.2 g.*

# Spinach Lasagna

*This healthier take on classic lasagna is light and wholesome, thanks to homemade lasagna noodles courtesy of your Marcato pasta maker. This meat-free delight is sure to be a hit with the whole family.*

*Servings: 9*
*Prep time: 45 minutes*
*Cook time: 60 minutes*

## Ingredients:

- 1 ball fresh egg pasta dough
- 1 16-ounce container whole milk ricotta
- 1/2 pound fresh spinach
- 1 cup parmesan, grated
- 1 egg
- 1 28-ounce can crushed tomatoes
- 1 pound low moisture mozzarella, grated
- 1 tablespoon dried oregano
- 1 tablespoon dried basil
- 1 tablespoon dried thyme
- 2 cloves garlic, finely chopped
- 2 tablespoons olive oil

## Directions:

1. Bring a large pot of water to a boil.
2. In a second pot, combine the tomatoes, oregano, basil, thyme, garlic, and olive oil over medium heat. Cook for 10 minutes and remove from heat.
3. Cut your pasta dough into quarters and use your Marcato pasta maker to roll them out to the #6 setting.
4. Blanch the spinach in the boiling water for 1 minute and then place in a food processor. Pulse until the spinach is finely chopped.

5. Coat the bottom of a casserole dish with tomato sauce and the add a layer of pasta sheets. Add a thin layer of spinach and about 6 small spoonfuls of ricotta cheese. Then add a thin layer of mozzarella cheese and other layer of sauce. Repeat this until you are out of ingredients.

6. Set your oven to 350°F and cover the casserole dish with foil. Bake for 35 minutes and then remove the foil and bake another 15 to 20 minutes.

*Nutritional Info: Calories: 335, Sodium: 694mg, Dietary Fiber: 3.8g, Total Fat: 20.6 g, Total Carbs: 13.6 g, Protein: 24.2 g.*

# Basil Fettuccini with a Garlic Lemon Sauce

*By adding a hint of fresh basil to your pasta dough you will create a flavorful canvas for a simple yet rich sauce.*

*Servings: 6*
*Prep time: 45 minutes*
*Cook time: 20 minutes*

## Ingredients:

2 cups all-purpose flour

6 egg yolks

4 tablespoons olive oil

1 teaspoon salt

4 cloves garlic

Juice of 2 lemons

1/4 fresh basil, finely chopped

Parmesan for topping

## Directions:

1. Start by making egg pasta dough but add the chopped basil when combining the eggs and flour. Allow the dough to rest for 30 minutes.
2. Boil a large pot of water.
3. Roll out your pasta dough to the #5 setting and cut with the fettuccini cutter.
4. In a medium saucepan add 3 tablespoons of olive oil and heat over medium heat. Add the garlic and cook until fragrant.
5. Add the pasta to the boiling water and cook 2 to 3 minutes, then strain.
6. Add the pasta to the pan with the garlic and add the lemon juice. Stir to coat the pasta and serve topped with parmesan cheese.

*Nutritional Info: Calories: 290, Sodium: 399mg, Dietary Fiber: 1.2 g, Total Fat: 14.3 g, Total Carbs: 33.5 g, Protein: 7.2 g.*

# Sun-Dried Tomato and Mushroom Linguini

*This rich vegetarian dish packs a lot of flavor thanks to robust sun-dried tomatoes and seasoned mushrooms. But the real star is homemade linguini from your Marcato pasta maker.*

*Servings: 8*
*Prep time: 45 minutes*
*Cook time: 20 minutes*

## Ingredients:

1 ball fresh egg pasta dough, quartered

2 tablespoons olive oil

8 ounces cremini mushrooms, sliced

3 cloves garlic, finely chopped

4 ounces. sun-dried tomatoes, chopped

1 cup chicken broth

1 cup dry white wine

1/2 cup heavy cream

1/2 cup parmesan cheese

1 tablespoon fresh basil, chopped

## Directions:

1. Bring a large pot of water to a boil.

2. Use your Marcato pasta maker to roll out your pasta dough to setting #5, and then use the linguini cutting attachment to cut the pasta. Dust with flour and set aside.

3. In a medium saucepan, heat the olive oil and add the mushrooms and garlic and cook for about 5 minutes. Then add the sun-dried tomatoes and cook another 3 minutes.

4. Add the wine and cook 5 minutes and then add the chicken broth. Cook until the liquid has reduced by half and then add the cream and parmesan cheese.

5. Boil the linguini for 2 to 3 minutes and strain.
6. Add the linguini to the pan with the sauce and stir to coat. Add the basil and serve.

*Nutritional Info: Calories: 114, Sodium: 186mg, Dietary Fiber: 0.7 g, Total Fat: 6.9 g, Total Carbs: 6.2 g, Protein: 2.3 g.*

# White Wine and Zucchini Fettuccini

*The addition of subtle herbs and wine allows this simple pasta recipe to highlight fresh egg pasta made with your Marcato pasta maker.*

*Servings: 8*
*Prep time: 45 minutes*
*Cook time: 20 minutes*

## Ingredients:

- 1 ball fresh egg pasta dough
- 2 large zucchinis
- 4 cloves garlic, smashed
- 1 cup dry white wine
- 1 teaspoon dried basil
- 1/4 cup Parmesan cheese
- 3 tablespoons olive oil

## Directions:

1. Bring a large pot of water to a boil.
2. Use your Marcato pasta maker to roll out your dough to the #5 setting, and use the fettuccini cutting attachment to cut the pasta.
3. In a medium saucepan, combine the oil and garlic over medium heat. Cook until the garlic just starts to brown, and add the wine.
4. Slice the zucchinis into thin disks and then quarter the disks. Add the zucchini to the saucepan and cook until they begin to soften and the wine has reduced by half.
5. Cook the pasta for 2 to 3 minutes and drain. Then add the pasta to the sauce and stir to coat. Toss in the parmesan cheese, stir, and serve.

*Nutritional Info: Calories: 105, Sodium: 36mg, Dietary Fiber: 1.1 g, Total Fat: 6 g, Total Carbs: 7.3 g, Protein: 1.6 g.*

# Mediterranean Spaghetti

*This Greek-inspired vegetarian pasta dish combines freshly made spaghetti with earthy flavors and plenty of fresh herbs.*

*Servings: 8*
*Prep time: 45 minutes*
*Cook time: 30 minutes*

## Ingredients:

*1 ball fresh egg or spinach pasta dough*

*1 cup artichokes in oil*

*1 cup black or Kalamata olives, pitted and halved*

*6 Roma tomatoes, roughly chopped*

*4 cloves garlic, finely chopped*

*1/4 red onion, finely chopped*

*3 tablespoons olive oil*

*1/4 cup dry white wine*

*1/2 cup feta cheese*

## Directions:

1. Bring a large pot of water to a boil.

2. Use your Marcato pasta maker to roll out your pasta dough to the #5 setting, and use the spaghetti cutting attachment to cut the pasta.

3. In a large saucepan, heat the oil over medium heat and add the garlic and wine. Reduce by half and then add the artichokes, tomatoes, olives, and onions. Cook until the artichokes are soft.

4. Boil the pasta for 2 to 3 minutes, drain and add to the sauce. Stir to coat. Toss in the feta cheese, stir again and serve.

*Nutritional Info: Calories: 143, Sodium: 268mg, Dietary Fiber: 2.3 g, Total Fat: 9.4 g, Total Carbs: 11.6 g, Protein: 3.7 g.*

# Spaghetti Pomodoro

*This light yet flavorful tomato sauce packs the rich flavor of fresh tomatoes and fresh garlic for a classic pasta dish that can be enjoyed anytime.*

*Servings: 4*
*Prep time: 30 minutes*
*Cook time: 30 minutes*

## Ingredients:

- 1/2 ball fresh egg pasta dough
- 1/4 cup extra virgin olive oil
- 1 shallot, minced
- 4 cloves garlic, minced
- 4 large ripe tomatoes, chopped
- 1/4 fresh basil, chopped
- 1/2 teaspoon sugar
- 1 teaspoon salt
- 1/2 teaspoon pepper
- 2 tablespoons butter

## Directions:

1. Bring a large pot of water to a boil.
2. Use your Marcato pasta maker to roll out your dough to the #5 setting. Then use the cutting attachment to cut the sheets into spaghetti.
3. In a large saucepan, heat the olive oil over medium heat and add the garlic and shallots. Cook until the shallots are fragrant and transparent.
4. Add the tomatoes, basil, salt, pepper, and sugar to the pan and cook until the tomatoes have softened.
5. Cook the spaghetti for 2 to 3 minutes, drain, and add to the saucepan. Then add the butter and stir to coat the pasta. Serve immediately.

*Nutritional Info: Calories: 221, Sodium: 658mg, Dietary Fiber: 2.4 g, Total Fat: 19.3 g, Total Carbs: 12.4 g, Protein: 2.5 g.*

# *Spaghetti alla Puttanesca*

*This spicy vegetarian pasta dish has become a favorite all over the world because of its big, balanced flavors. This recipe adds the extra authentic flavor of fresh egg spaghetti.*

*Servings: 8*
*Prep time: 30 minutes*
*Cook time: 30 minutes*

## Ingredients:

- *1 ball fresh egg spaghetti*
- *5 cloves garlic, finely chopped*
- *2 teaspoons anchovy paste*
- *1/2 teaspoon red pepper flakes*
- *1/3 cup extra virgin olive oil*
- *1 28-ounce can crushed San Marzano tomatoes*
- *1/2 cup Kalamata olives, pitted*
- *2 tablespoons capers*
- *1/2 teaspoon sugar*
- *1/2 cup fresh basil, chopped*

## Directions:

1. Bring a large pot of water to a boil.

2. Use your Marcato pasta maker to roll out your pasta dough to the #5 setting. Then use the spaghetti cutting attachment to cut the pasta sheets.

3. In a large saucepan, heat the oil over medium heat and add the garlic. Cook until garlic is fragrant, then add the tomatoes, olives, anchovy paste, red pepper flakes, salt, and sugar.

4. Boil the spaghetti for 2 to 3 minutes, drain and add to the saucepan. Stir to coat and then serve topped with fresh basil.

*Nutritional Info: Calories: 238, Sodium: 1653mg, Dietary Fiber: 4.2 g, Total Fat: 11.5 g, Total Carbs: 31.1 g, Protein: 8.5 g.*

# Linguini with Creamy Butternut Squash Sauce

*This comforting cream sauce is made with rich butternut squash for a flavor that is perfect for fall.*

*Servings: 8*
*Prep time: 45 minutes*
*Cook time: 30 minutes*

## Ingredients:

- 1 ball fresh egg pasta dough
- 2 tablespoons olive oil
- 1 tablespoon fresh sage, finely chopped
- 1 large butternut squash, peeled and cut into chunks
- 1 medium yellow onion, finely chopped
- 2 cloves garlic, finely chopped
- 1/4 teaspoon red pepper flakes
- 1/2 teaspoon salt
- 2 cups chicken or vegetable broth
- 1/2 cup Parmesan cheese, grated, for topping

## Directions:

1. Bring a large pot of water to a boil.
2. Using your Marcato pasta maker, roll out your pasta dough to the #4 setting. Then use the linguini cutting attachment to cut the sheets.
3. In a large saucepan, heat the oil over medium heat and add the garlic and onions. Season with salt and pepper and cook until the onions are translucent.
4. Add the squash, red pepper flakes, sage, and broth. Cook until the liquid has reduced and the squash is soft. Remove from heat.
5. Once the squash mixture has cooled slightly, transfer it to a blender and puree until smooth.

6. Boil the pasta for 3 to 4 minutes and drain.

7. In the original saucepan, combine the pasta, squash puree, and 1/3 cup of pasta cooking liquid. Stir to coat, and serve topped with grated parmesan cheese.

*Nutritional Info: Calories: 120, Sodium: 199mg, Dietary Fiber: 1.4 g, Total Fat: 5.3 g, Total Carbs: 6.9 g, Protein: 11.3g.*

# Roasted Cauliflower Spaghetti Marinara

*Cauliflower is a great substitute for meat and cheese, and this recipe pairs delicious roasted cauliflower with tangy marinara for a robust punch of flavor and nutrition.*

*Servings: 8*
*Prep time: 30 minutes*
*Cook time: 1 hour*

## Ingredients:

1 ball fresh egg pasta dough

1 head cauliflower, sliced

1 28-ounce can San Marzano crushed tomatoes

1/3 cup olive oil

4 cloves garlic, chopped

1 medium yellow onion, chopped

1 tablespoon fresh oregano, finely chopped

2 tablespoons fresh basil, finely chopped

Salt and black pepper

1/2 cup parmesan cheese, grated

## Directions:

1. Bring a large pot of water to a boil, and preheat your oven to 400°F.

2. Use your Marcato pasta maker to roll out the dough to the #5 thickness. Then use the spaghetti cutting attachment to cut the sheets.

3. In a large saucepan, heat the oil over medium heat and add the garlic and onions. Cook until the onions are translucent.

4. Add the tomatoes, oregano, and basil, and simmer for 10 to 15 minutes.

5. Place the slices of cauliflower on a baking sheet and drizzle with olive oil, sprinkle with salt and pepper and parmesan cheese. Place in the oven for 15 to 20 minutes.

6. Cook the pasta for 2 to 3 minutes, drain and add to the pan with the sauce along with 1/4 cup of the pasta cooking liquid. Stir to coat. Serve pasta topped with slices of roasted cauliflower.

*Nutritional Info: Calories: 233, Sodium: 1473mg, Dietary Fiber: 5 g, Total Fat: 9.1 g, Total Carbs: 31.7 g, Protein: 8.5 g.*

# Linguini with Eggplant and Miso Butter

*This sophisticated pasta dish uses roasted eggplant and miso paste to create new and interesting flavors that will still allow your fresh pasta to shine.*

*Servings: 8*
*Prep time: 30 minutes*
*Cook time: 45 minutes*

## Ingredients:

*1 ball fresh egg pasta dough*

*1 large eggplant, peeled and chopped into chunks*

*3 tablespoons olive oil*

*6 tablespoons butter*

*2 tablespoons white miso paste*

*Ground black pepper*

*1/2 cup grated parmesan cheese*

## Directions:

1. Bring a large pot of water to a boil, and preheat your oven to 425°F.

2. Place eggplant chunks on a baking sheet and drizzle with olive oil and season with black pepper. Bake for 30 minutes.

3. Use your Marcato pasta maker to roll your pasta dough to the #4 setting and then use the linguini attachment to cut the sheets.

4. In a small saucepan, heat the butter until it begins to brown, whisking the whole time. Remove from heat and season with pepper and add the miso paste.

5. Cook the linguini for 3 to 4 minutes, drain and then combine with the miso sauce. Remove the eggplant from the oven and toss with the pasta. Top with grated parmesan.

*Nutritional Info: Calories: 203, Sodium: 261mg, Dietary Fiber: 2.2 g, Total Fat: 17.7 g, Total Carbs: 7.6 g, Protein: 5.9 g.*

# Arugula Walnut Pesto

*This fun take on classic pesto sauce will work with any type of pasta you choose to make, from simple spaghetti to farfalle or fusilli.*

*Servings: 6*
*Prep time: 30 minutes*
*Cook time: 45 minutes*

## Ingredients:

4 cups arugula leaves, stems removed

1 cup walnuts

1 cup parmesan cheese, grated

1 cup extra virgin olive oil

12 cloves garlic

1 teaspoon salt

Juice of 1 lemon

## Directions:

1. In a medium saucepan, heat 2 tablespoons of olive oil and over medium heat and add the whole garlic cloves. Cook until they just begin to brown and remove from heat. Remove the garlic from the pan and add the walnuts. Toast the nuts over medium heat until they are fragrant.

2. In a food processor, combine the arugula, walnuts, garlic, and salt. Pulse the food processor and slowly add the oil. Process until smooth, then stir in the parmesan cheese. When that is blended, add the lemon juice and enjoy with your choice of pasta.

*Nutritional Info: Calories: 551, Sodium: 739mg, Dietary Fiber: 1.8 g, Total Fat: 54 g, Total Carbs: 6.6 g, Protein: 17.8 g.*

# Roasted Red Pepper Fettuccini

*This sweet and smoky fettuccini dish is fresh tasting yet hearty, and your fresh pasta provides the perfect canvas for this sophisticated sauce.*

*Servings: 8*
*Prep time: 30 minutes*
*Cook time: 45 minutes*

## Ingredients:

1 ball fresh egg or spinach pasta dough

3 red bell peppers, cut into large slices

1/2 teaspoon red pepper flakes

1 teaspoon fresh oregano, finely chopped

2 cloves garlic, finely chopped

1/3 cup olive oil

Juice from 1 lemon

Salt and black pepper

## Directions:

1. Bring a large pot of water to a boil, and preheat your oven to 450°F.

2. Use your Marcato pasta maker to roll out your pasta dough to the #5 setting. Then use the fettuccini cutting attachment to cut the sheets.

3. Lay out the red pepper sliced on a baking sheet, drizzle with olive oil and season with salt and pepper. Cook the peppers in the oven for about 20 minutes.

4. When the peppers have finished roasting, place half of them in a blender with the remaining olive oil, garlic, red pepper flakes, oregano, and lemon juice. Blend until smooth.

5. Cook the pasta for 2 to 3 minutes, drain and place in a pan with the pepper puree. Stir to coat and serve topped with the whole peppers.

*Nutritional Info: Calories: 99, Sodium: 2 mg, Dietary Fiber: 0.8 g, Total Fat: 8.6 g, Total Carbs: 6.1 g, Protein: 0.9 g.*

# 9

## MEAT RECIPES

# Classic Bolognese

*This classic sauce combines slow-cooked tomatoes with rich meat to produce a comforting, traditional bolognese that the entire family with love. Make it with spaghetti, fettuccini, or any pasta shape you like.*

Servings: 6
Prep time: 30 minutes
Cook time: 4 hours

## Ingredients:

- 1 tablespoon olive oil
- 3 tablespoons butter
- 1/2 cup onion, chopped
- 2/3 cup celery, chopped
- 2/3 cup carrot, chopped
- 1/2 pound ground beef
- 1/2 pound ground pork
- 1/2 pound ground lamb
- 1/2 cup chicken livers, pureed
- 1 cup whole milk
- 1 cup dry red wine
- 1 28-ounce can San Marzano tomatoes, crushed
- Salt and black pepper

## Directions:

1. In a Dutch oven or large pot, heat the oil over medium heat and add all of the meat except the liver. Brown and remove from the pot.
2. Add the butter and onion to the pot and cook until the onion is translucent. Then add the celery and carrot.
3. Add the milk and browned meat and simmer for a few minutes, then add the wine and simmer for another 10 minutes. Add the tomatoes and season with salt and pepper.

4. Add the chicken livers, stir and allow the sauce to simmer on low heat for at least 3 hours. Serve with your choice of pasta - wide, flat noodles work well.

*Nutritional Info: Calories: 377, Sodium: 167 mg, Dietary Fiber: 2.3 g, Total Fat: 16.9 g, Total Carbs: 10.6 g, Protein: 37.7 g.*

# Spaghetti alla Carbonara

*This rich and satisfying classic meat pasta uses bacon and eggs to achieve a flavor that will pair perfectly with spaghetti made with your Marcato pasta maker.*

*Servings: 4*
*Prep time: 15 minutes*
*Cook time: 30 minutes*

## Ingredients:

- 1/2 ball fresh egg pasta dough
- 2 large whole eggs
- 2 egg yolks
- 1/2 pound bacon or pancetta, diced
- 1 tablespoon olive oil
- 1/3 cup parmesan cheese
- 1/3 cup Romano cheese
- Salt and black pepper

## Directions:

1. Bring a large pot of water to a boil.
2. In a large bowl, combine the eggs, parmesan, and Romano cheese with a pinch of salt and pepper.
3. In a large skillet, cook the meat until the fat has rendered. Remove from heat and set aside.
4. Use your Marcato pasta maker to roll out dough to the #5 setting and use the spaghetti attachment to cut the sheets.
5. Cook pasta for 2 to 3 minutes and drain.
6. Reheat the meat and add the pasta to the pan. Then add the cheese and egg mixture. Stir and remove from heat. Serve topped with Parmesan cheese.

*Nutritional Info: Calories: 212, Sodium: 402 mg, Dietary Fiber: 0.1 g, Total Fat: 15.9 g, Total Carbs: 4.6 g, Protein: 12.8 g.*

# Pasta with Ricotta Meatballs

*These are perhaps the richest, most flavorful meatballs on Earth. Combined with pasta from your Marcato pasta maker, this is a dish that will have everyone begging for more.*

*Servings: 8*
*Prep time: 30 minutes*
*Cook time: 60 minutes*

## Ingredients:

- *1/2 onion, finely chopped*
- *2 tablespoons olive oil*
- *6 cloves garlic, finely chopped*
- *1 pound ground beef*
- *1 cup whole milk ricotta*
- *1/4 cup Italian parsley, finely chopped*
- *1 egg, beaten*
- *1/8 teaspoon cayenne pepper*
- *1/3 cup dry bread crumbs*
- *1 28-ounce can San Marzano tomatoes, pureed*
- *1/4 cup fresh basil, chopped*
- *1 cup water*
- *Salt and black pepper*

## Directions:

1. In a medium saucepan, heat 2 tablespoons of olive oil and cook the onions until they are translucent. Stir in half of the garlic and cook several more minutes, then remove from heat.

2. In a large bowl, stir together the ground beef, ricotta, parsley, egg, salt and pepper, cayenne pepper, and add the onion mixture. Stir until combined, then add the breadcrumbs.

3. In a large saucepan, combine the tomatoes with the basil and remaining garlic. Cook for about 10 to 15 minutes.

4. Roll about 2 tablespoons of meat mixture into balls and heat remaining olive oil in a large skillet. Brown the meatballs on all sides and remove from heat.

5. Add the meatballs to the tomato sauce and simmer on low heat for about 30 minutes. Serve with pasta from your Marcato pasta maker.

*Nutritional Info: Calories: 213, Sodium: 98 mg, Dietary Fiber: 1.7 g, Total Fat: 10.1 g, Total Carbs: 9.2 g, Protein: 21.4 g.*

# Chicken Piccata with Capellini

*This traditional chicken dish pairs perfectly with freshly made angel hair pasta from your Marcato pasta maker.*

*Servings: 4*
*Prep time: 30 minutes*
*Cook time: 45 minutes*

## Ingredients:

*1/2 ball fresh egg pasta dough*
*1 pound boneless chicken breasts, pounded thin*
*1 cup dry white wine*
*1/3 cup chicken broth*
*Juice from 2 lemons*
*1/3 cup flour*
*1/4 teaspoon paprika*
*2 tablespoons olive oil*
*2 cloves garlic, minced*
*2 tablespoons capers*
*2 tablespoons fresh parsley, chopped*
*Salt and black pepper*

## Directions:

1. In a shallow dish, combine the flour, pepper, and paprika. Dredge the chicken in the flour mixture. Then add the chicken to the pan and cook until browned.

2. In a large skillet, heat the olive oil and add the garlic, cooking until golden brown. Remove from heat.

3. Boil a large pot of water, and use your Marcato pasta maker to roll out the dough to the #6 setting and use the capellini cutting attachment to cut the sheets.

4. Heat a large skillet and add the wine, cooking until reduced by half. Add the chicken broth, capers, garlic, and lemon juice. Add the chicken and cook until the sauce has thickened.

5. Cook the pasta for about 2 minutes, drain and add to the skillet with the sauce. Stir to coat and serve.

*Nutritional Info: Calories: 397, Sodium: 319 mg, Dietary Fiber: 0.8 g, Total Fat: 16.3 g, Total Carbs: 15.9 g, Protein: 35.2 g.*

# One Pot Chicken Pasta

*This quick and easy one-pot pasta dish is perfect on a winter night, and thanks to your Marcato pasta maker, it will feature perfectly made pasta.*

*Servings: 4*
*Prep time: 10 minutes*
*Cook time: 30 minutes*

## Ingredients:

*1/2 ball fresh egg pasta dough*

*4 skinless chicken breasts, cubed*

*2 cloves garlic, chopped*

*1/2 cup red wine*

*1 28-ounce can San Marzano tomatoes*

*1 cup fresh spinach, chopped*

*1 cup mozzarella cheese, shredded*

## Directions:

1. Bring a large pot of water to a boil.

2. Use your Marcato pasta maker to roll out your dough to the #5 setting then use the fettuccini attachment to cut the sheets. Then cut the fettuccini into 2-inch-long pieces. Boil the pasta for 2 to 3 minutes, drain, and set aside.

3. In a large skillet, heat the olive oil and add the garlic, and chicken, cooking for 5 to 8 minutes. Add the wine and tomatoes and stir while cooking.

4. Add the cooked pasta to the skillet and add the spinach and mozzarella, simmering until the cheese has melted.

*Nutritional Info: Calories: 218, Sodium: 136 mg, Dietary Fiber: 2.7 g, Total Fat: 4.8 g, Total Carbs: 12.8 g, Protein: 25.8 g.*

# Ham and Leek Pasta

*Fresh leeks are packed with complex flavors and pair perfectly with country ham and freshly made pasta.*

*Servings: 4*
*Prep time: 15 minutes*
*Cook time: 20 minutes*

## Ingredients:

*1/2 ball fresh egg pasta dough*

*2 tablespoons butter*

*1 large leek, chopped*

*2 cups fresh or frozen peas*

*1 cup half and half*

*1/2 pound country ham, diced*

*1/2 cup Parmesan cheese*

## Directions:

1. Bring a pot of water to a boil, and use your Marcato pasta maker to roll out dough to the #5 setting. Then use the spaghetti attachment to cut the sheets.

2. In a large skillet, melt the butter and add the leeks, cooking until soft. Then add the peas and half and half, bring to a boil, and simmer until thickened.

3. Boil the pasta for 2 to 3 minutes, drain, and add to the skillet. Stir to coat with sauce and serve topped with parmesan cheese.

*Nutritional Info: Calories: 408, Sodium: 1153 mg, Dietary Fiber: 5.7 g, Total Fat: 24.5 g, Total Carbs: 23.6 g, Protein: 25.2 g.*

# Pepper Steak Pasta

*This hearty dish is excellent when paired with wide pasta made with your Marcato pasta maker.*

*Servings: 6*
*Prep time: 20 minutes*
*Cook time: 30 minutes*

## Ingredients:

*1 ball fresh egg pasta dough*

*1 pound top sirloin or New York strip steak, cut into slices*

*2 tablespoons vegetable oil*

*1 red bell pepper*

*1 green bell pepper*

*1/2 onion, sliced*

*2 tablespoons tomato paste*

*1/2 can San Marzano tomatoes, crushed*

*2 tablespoons soy sauce*

*Salt and black pepper*

## Directions:

1. Bring a large pot of water to a boil, and use your Marcato pasta maker to roll out your dough to the #5 setting. Then use the fettuccini attachment to cut the sheets.

2. Season the steak with salt and pepper. Heat the oil in a large skillet and add the steak. Cook until just browned and remove from the pan.

3. Add the peppers, onions, tomatoes, tomato paste, and soy sauce to the pan and cook until soft.

4. Cook the pasta for 2 to 3 minutes, drain, and add to the skillet. Return the steak to the skillet and stir.

*Nutritional Info: Calories: 228, Sodium: 391 mg, Dietary Fiber: 1.2 g, Total Fat: 10.1 g, Total Carbs: 9.1 g, Protein: 24.6 g.*

# Spaghetti with Sausage and Tomatoes

*This slightly spicy dish uses fresh sausage and tomatoes to create a sophisticated yet easy-to-make dish.*

*Servings: 8*
*Prep time: 15 minutes*
*Cook time: 30 minutes*

## Ingredients:

- *1 ball fresh egg pasta dough*
- *1 tablespoon olive oil*
- *1 pound hot Italian sausage, chopped*
- *1 medium onion, chopped*
- *4 cloves garlic, finely chopped*
- *1 1/2 cups chicken broth*
- *1 teaspoon dried basil*
- *2 large tomatoes, diced*
- *1 cup fresh spinach, chopped*
- *1/2 cup parmesan cheese*

## Directions:

1. Bring a large pot of water to a boil, and use your Marcato pasta maker to roll out your dough to the #5 setting. Use the spaghetti cutter to cut the sheets.

2. In a large skillet, heat the oil and add the sausage, cooking until no longer pink. Add the onion and garlic and cook until they are translucent. Then add the broth, basil, and tomatoes. Cook for 5 to 10 minutes or until everything is soft. Then add the spinach.

3. Cook the pasta, drain, and add to the skillet, stirring to coat. Serve pasta topped with Parmesan cheese.

*Nutritional Info: Calories: 241, Sodium: 580 mg, Dietary Fiber: 1 g, Total Fat: 18.3 g, Total Carbs: 5.5 g, Protein: 13.1 g.*

# Classic Beef Stroganoff

*This hearty, classic favorite is made even more rich and satisfying with wide pappardelle made fresh with your Marcato pasta maker.*

*Servings: 4*
*Prep time: 20 minutes*
*Cook time: 20 minutes*

## Ingredients:

1/2 ball fresh egg pasta dough

1 pound filet mignon, cut into strips

5 tablespoons butter

1/3 cup shallots, chopped

1/2 pound cremini mushrooms, thinly sliced

Salt and black pepper

1/2 teaspoon tarragon

1 cup sour cream

## Directions:

1. Bring a large pot of water to a boil.

2. Use your Marcato pasta maker to roll out dough to the #6 setting. Use a large knife to cut the sheets into 1-inch-wide strips.

3. In a large skillet, melt 3 tablespoons of butter, and quickly brown the strips of filet. Add salt and pepper as you cook. Remove the beef from the pan.

4. Add the shallots to the pan and cook until translucent. Remove from the pan.

5. Add the rest of the butter to the pan and cook the mushrooms until they become soft, about 5 minutes. Add the tarragon to the mushrooms.

6. Add the sour cream, beef, and shallots back the pan with the mushrooms. Do not boil.

7. Boil the pasta for 2 to 3 minutes, drain, and add to the pan with the sauce.

*Nutritional Info: Calories: 488, Sodium: 211 mg, Dietary Fiber: 0.4 g, Total Fat: 34.4 g, Total Carbs: 8.8 g, Protein: 36 g.*

# Spicy Lamb and Fennel Fettuccini

*This spicy lamb meat sauce is perfect for a wide noodle like fettuccini and has a spicy kick that is delicious and exciting.*

*Servings: 8*

*Prep time: 30 minutes*

*Cook time: 20 minutes*

## Ingredients:

- *1 ball fresh egg pasta dough*
- *1 28-ounce can crushed tomatoes*
- *1 pound ground lamb*
- *3 cloves garlic, chopped*
- *1 tablespoon fennel seeds*
- *1 tablespoon fresh oregano*
- *3 tablespoons olive oil*
- *1 teaspoon red pepper flakes*
- *1/2 cup red wine*
- *Salt and black pepper*
- *Parmesan cheese*

## Directions:

1. Bring a large pot of water to a boil, and use your Marcato pasta maker to roll out dough to the #5 setting. Use the fettuccini attachment to cut the sheets.
2. In a large skillet, heat the oil and add the lamb, fennel seeds, salt and pepper, over high heat.
3. When the lamb is browned, add the wine and garlic. Cook until slightly reduced and add the tomatoes, oregano, and pepper flakes. Simmer for 10 to 15 minutes.
4. Cook the pasta for 2 to 3 minutes, drain and add to the skillet with the sauce. Add 1/4 cup of the cooking liquid. Stir well and served topped with parmesan cheese.

*Nutritional Info: Calories: 230, Sodium: 274 mg, Dietary Fiber: 3.8 g, Total Fat: 10.5 g, Total Carbs: 11.4 g, Protein: 20.1 g.*

# Linguini with Chicken and Prosciutto

*This light but flavorful pasta combines chicken with savory prosciutto to create a well-balanced and satisfying dish that doesn't take much time to prepare.*

*Servings: 4*
*Prep time: 10 minutes*
*Cook time: 25 minutes*

## Ingredients:

- 1/2 ball fresh egg pasta dough
- 1 tablespoon olive oil
- 1/2 pound prosciutto, chopped
- 3/4 pound boneless chicken breasts, cut into small strips
- 2 teaspoons dried oregano
- 2 cloves garlic, minced
- 1 head broccoli, finely chopped
- 3/4 cup whole milk
- Salt and black pepper
- 1 cup parmesan or asiago cheese

## Directions:

1. Bring a large pot of water to a boil, and use your Marcato pasta maker to roll out your dough to the #5 setting. Then use the linguini cutting attachment to cut the sheets.

2. In a large skillet, heat the oil over medium heat. Add the chicken and season with salt and pepper. Add the oregano and cook until the chicken is no longer pink. Remove from the pan.

3. Add the garlic to the skillet and cook until fragrant. Add the broccoli and 1/4 cup water and cook until the broccoli is tender.

4. Boil the pasta for 3 to 4 minutes, drain and set aside.

5. Add the milk to the skillet and toss in the chicken and prosciutto. Then add the pasta to the skillet with the cheese. Stir until the cheese has melted and serve.

*Nutritional Info: Calories: 340, Sodium: 847mg, Dietary Fiber: 0.5 g, Total Fat: 16.2 g, Total Carbs: 6.2 g, Protein: 40.9 g.*

# Spaghetti with Sausage and Radicchio

*This fresh take on a classic spaghetti is bright and refreshing for times when you want pasta, but you don't want a heavy dish.*

*Servings: 4*
*Prep time: 10 minutes*
*Cook time: 25 minutes*

## Ingredients:

- 1/2 ball fresh egg pasta dough
- 3 tablespoons olive oil
- 1/2 red onion, finely chopped
- 1/4 cup fresh mint leaves,
- 2 bay leaves
- 2 sweet Italian sausages, casings removed and chopped
- 3/4 cup dry white wine
- 1/2 head radicchio, thinly sliced
- Salt and black pepper
- 1/4 cup parmesan cheese, grated

## Directions:

1. Bring a large pot of water to a boil, and use your Marcato pasta maker to roll out your dough to the #5 setting. Then use the spaghetti cutting attachment to cut the sheets.

2. In a large skillet, heat the oil over medium heat, add the onion, sausage, mint, and bay leaves.

3. Once the sausage is browned, add the wine and stir until it has reduced slightly. Add some salt and pepper.

4. Cook the pasta in the boiling water for 2 to 3 minutes, drain, and add to the pan with the sauce. Add the radicchio and parmesan cheese and serve.

*Nutritional Info: Calories: 204, Sodium: 249 mg, Dietary Fiber: 0.8 g, Total Fat: 14.2 g, Total Carbs: 5 g, Protein: 7.4 g.*

# Grandma's Spaghetti with Red Sauce and Meatballs

*This favorite of Italian grandmothers everywhere is a simple and satisfying dish that everyone will love for any occasion.*

*Servings: 8*
*Prep time: 30 minutes*
*Cook time: 1 hour*

## Ingredients:

- 1 ball fresh egg pasta dough
- 2 large eggs, beaten
- 1/2 cup milk
- 1 cup breadcrumbs
- 2 pounds ground beef
- 1 cup onion, finely chopped
- 2 tablespoons parsley, chopped
- 3 garlic cloves, crushed
- Salt and black pepper
- 1/4 cup olive oil
- 2 tablespoons sugar
- 1 tablespoon dried basil
- 1 teaspoon fennel seeds
- 1/4 teaspoon pepper
- 1 28-ounce can crushed tomatoes
- 1 12-ounce can tomato paste
- 1 cup parmesan cheese, grated

## Directions:

1. Bring a large pot of water to a boil, and use your Marcato pasta maker to roll out your dough to the #5 setting. Then use the spaghetti cutting attachment to cut the sheets.

2. In a large bowl, combine the eggs, milk, and breadcrumbs. Let stand 5 minutes, then add the beef, half the onion, parsley, 1 clove of garlic, salt and pepper. Mix well and form 24 meatballs.

3. In a large pot or Dutch oven, heat the oil and cook the remaining onion and garlic until golden brown. Add the tomatoes, basil, fennel, tomato paste, salt and pepper, and stir well. Simmer for 1 hour.

4. Boil the pasta for 2 to 3 minutes, and drain.

5. In a large skillet, brown the meatballs and make sure they are cooked through. Then add the meatballs to the sauce and serve with the spaghetti.

*Nutritional Info: Calories: 443, Sodium: 442 mg, Dietary Fiber: 6 g, Total Fat: 16.1 g, Total Carbs: 31.9 g, Protein: 43.2 g.*

# Tagliatelle with Heart Vodka Sauce

*This rich take on a classic vodka cream sauce is perfect for warming up on a cold day, and the hand-cut tagliatelle is perfect for a rich cream sauce.*

*Servings: 8*
*Prep time: 10 minutes*
*Cook time: 30 minutes*

## Ingredients:

- 1 ball fresh egg pasta dough
- 1/2 cup butter
- 1 onion, diced
- 1 cup vodka
- 2 28-ounce cans crushed tomatoes
- 1 pint heavy cream
- 1 pound sweet Italian sausage
- 1/2 cup parmesan cheese

## Directions:

1. Bring a large pot of water to a boil, and use your Marcato pasta maker to roll out your dough to the #6 setting. Use a large knife to cut the sheets into 1 inch wide strips.

2. In a large skillet, melt the butter over medium heat and add the onion, cooking until just slightly browned. Add the sausage and cook until browned.

3. Add the vodka and cook for 10 minutes, then add the tomatoes and cook for 30 minutes. Pour in the heavy cream and stir for 30 seconds.

4. Boil the pasta for 3 to 4 minutes, drain and add to the skillet with the sauce. Stir to coat and serve topped with Parmesan.

*Nutritional Info: Calories: 567, Sodium: 876 mg, Dietary Fiber: 6.6 g, Total Fat: 40 g, Total Carbs: 20.7 g, Protein: 17.8 g.*

# Fettuccini with Pancetta Cream Sauce

*This mild, smooth, creamy sauce coats every strand of pasta to make a dish that is sure to become a family favorite.*

*Servings: 4*
*Prep time: 10 minutes*
*Cook time: 30*

## Ingredients:

- 1/2 ball fresh egg pasta dough
- 2 tablespoons butter
- 2 tablespoons garlic, chopped
- 2 tablespoons shallots, chopped
- 1/2 pound pancetta, diced
- 4 tablespoons white wine
- 2 cups half and half
- 4 eggs, beaten
- Salt and black pepper
- 1/2 cup parmesan cheese, grated

## Directions:

1. Bring a large pot of water to a boil, and use your Marcato pasta maker to roll out your dough to the #5 setting. Then use the fettuccini cutting attachment to cut the sheets.
2. In a large skillet, melt butter over medium heat, add the garlic and shallots and cook until slightly browned.
3. Add the pancetta and cook for 2 minutes, stirring often. Add the wine and cook until it has reduced slightly.
4. Add the half and half, reduce heat, and simmer until the sauce has thickened slightly.
5. Cook the pasta for 2 to 3 minutes, drain and return to the pasta pot.

6. Pour the cream sauce and the eggs into the pasta pot and cook on low heat for 2 minutes, while coating the pasta with sauce. Serve topped with parmesan cheese.

*Nutritional Info: Calories: 467, Sodium: 895 mg, Dietary Fiber: 0.1 g, Total Fat: 37.8 g, Total Carbs: 8.6 g, Protein: 21.1 g.*

# Chicken Milano

*This simple, traditional dish is easy to make and packs plenty of flavor. Try it with freshly made fettuccini or any other shape of pasta.*

*Servings: 4*

*Prep time: 20 minutes*

*Cook time: 30 minutes*

## Ingredients:

*1/2 ball fresh egg pasta dough*

*1 tablespoon butter*

*2 cloves garlic, minced*

*1/2 cup sun-dried tomatoes, chopped*

*1 cup chicken broth*

*1 cup heavy cream*

*1 pound boneless chicken breasts*

*2 tablespoons olive oil*

*2 tablespoons fresh basil*

*Salt and black pepper*

## Directions:

1. Bring a large pot of water to a boil, and use your Marcato pasta maker to roll out your dough to the #5 setting. Then use the fettuccini cutting attachment to cut the sheets.
2. In a large saucepan, melt the butter over low heat, add the garlic and cook for 1 minute. Add the tomatoes and half the chicken broth. Bring to a boil. Reduce heat and simmer for 10 minutes. Add the cream, bring to a boil and stir until thickened.
3. In a large skillet, heat the oil, and season the chicken with salt and pepper. Cook the chicken and transfer to a cutting board.
4. In the same skillet, add the rest of the chicken broth, reduce slightly and add the cream sauce and the basil.
5. Boil the pasta for 2 to 3 minutes, drain and divide onto 4 plates. Top with a chicken breast and 3 to 4 tablespoons of the sauce.

*Nutritional Info: Calories: 423, Sodium: 323 mg, Dietary Fiber: 0.3 g, Total Fat: 29.8 g, Total Carbs: 2.9 g, Protein: 35.1 g.*

# *Cajun Steak Spaghetti*

*This hearty, spicy pasta dish uses Cajun flavors to create a pasta unlike anything you've had before.*

*Servings: 6*
*Prep time: 15 minutes*
*Cook time: 30 minutes*

## Ingredients:

*1 ball fresh egg pasta dough*

*2 pounds sirloin steak*

*1 1/2 teaspoons fennel seed, crushed*

*2 teaspoons dried oregano*

*1/2 teaspoon red pepper flakes*

*1 teaspoon paprika*

*1 teaspoon black pepper*

*1 teaspoon salt*

*2 tablespoons butter*

*1/4 cup minced garlic*

*1/2 red onion, minced*

*1/2 cup parmesan cheese, grated*

## Directions:

1. Bring a large pot of water to a boil, and use your Marcato pasta maker to roll out your dough to the #5 setting. Then use the spaghetti cutting attachment to cut the sheets.

2. In a spice mill, combine the fennel seed, oregano, pepper flakes, paprika, salt, and pepper, and mix well. Coat the steaks with the spice rub.

3. In a large skillet, melt the butter and cook the garlic and onion until tender.

4. Boil the pasta for 2 to 3 minutes, drain, and add to the skillet.

5. Grill the steak over high heat and transfer to a cutting board. Allow to rest for 5 minutes, then slice and add to the skillet. Stir well and top with parmesan cheese.

*Nutritional Info: Calories: 336, Sodium: 520 mg, Dietary Fiber: 1 g, Total Fat: 13.6 g, Total Carbs: 4.4 g, Protein: 46.8 g.*

# Delicata Squash Carbonara

*This well-balanced carbonara uses sweet Delicata squash for a delightful spaghetti dish that is perfect any time of year.*

*Servings: 6*
*Prep time: 30 minutes*
*Cook time: 60 minutes*

## Ingredients:

- *1 ball fresh egg pasta dough*
- *2 medium Delicata squash*
- *2 tablespoons olive oil*
- *1/2 pound pancetta, chopped*
- *6 egg yolks*
- *2 teaspoons lemon zest*
- *1/2 cup parmesan cheese*

## Directions:

1. Bring a large pot of water to a boil, and use your Marcato pasta maker to roll out your dough to the #5 setting. Then use the spaghetti cutting attachment to cut the sheets.

2. Preheat oven to 350°F. Slice the squash lengthwise, scrape out seeds, and cut into 1/4-inch-thick disks. Brush with olive oil and season with salt and pepper. Place on a baking sheet with chopped pancetta and roast until squash is tender

3. Boil the pasta for 2 to 3 minutes and drain.

4. Add pasta to the skillet. Lightly beat the eggs and combine with the zest. Toss the pasta with the egg mixture and the pancetta mixture in the skillet and cook until slightly thickened. Serve topped with parmesan cheese.

*Nutritional Info: Calories: 327, Sodium: 927 mg, Dietary Fiber: 0.4 g, Total Fat: 26 g, Total Carbs: 2 g, Protein: 18.7 g.*

# *Eggplant and Prosciutto Ragu*

*This hearty sauce can be paired with any type of pasta, but we recommend using your Marcato pasta maker to make a wide, flat noodle like fettuccini or tagliatelle.*

*Servings: 4*
*Prep time: 20 minutes*
*Cook time: 60 minutes*

## Ingredients:

*8 tablespoons olive oil*

*2 small eggplants, cut into 1/2-inch cubes*

*1/2 pound prosciutto, chopped*

*1 small onion, finely chopped*

*2 cloves garlic, chopped*

*1 tablespoon tomato paste*

*1/2 cup tomato puree*

*1 tablespoon fish sauce*

*2 tablespoons butter*

*1/4 cup parmesan cheese, grated*

## Directions:

1. In a large pot, heat 3 tablespoons of oil over medium heat. Add the eggplant seasoned with salt and pepper. Stir until the eggplant has softened, about 5 to 6 minutes. Remove from heat.

2. In the same skillet, add the prosciutto, onion, and garlic. Cook until the onion has softened.

3. Add the tomato paste and tomato puree, cooking until it has slightly darkened. Add the eggplant and 1 cup water. Reduce heat to medium and cook until sauce has thickened. Serve with your choice of pasta.

*Nutritional Info: Calories: 450, Sodium: 1151 mg, Dietary Fiber: 5.2 g, Total Fat: 38.7 g, Total Carbs: 13.7 g, Protein: 16.5 g.*

# Beef Short Rib Ragu

*This ultimate beef ragu is made with tender short ribs and is slow cooked for amazing flavor and texture. It pairs well with any pasta made with your Marcato pasta maker.*

*Servings: 8*
*Prep time: 8 hours*
*Cook time: 4 to 6 hours*

## Ingredients:

- 4 beef short ribs
- 3 cups red wine
- 2 tablespoons olive oil
- 2 onions, chopped
- 4 cloves garlic, chopped
- 1 large carrot, chopped
- 1 celery stalk, chopped
- 2 tablespoons tomato paste
- 1 gallon beef stock
- 2 28-ounce cans crushed tomatoes
- 4 sprigs rosemary
- 1 bay leaf

## Directions:

1. In a plastic container, combine the ribs and wine. Cover and place in the refrigerator overnight.

2. Pre-heat oven to 300°F. In a Dutch oven, heat the oil over medium heat. Remove the ribs from the wine, pat dry, and cook until browned on all sides. Remove the ribs.

3. Add the vegetables and tomato paste, stirring until everything has softened. Add the wine and reduce by half, then add the stock 2 cups at a time, reducing by half between each addition of stock. Add the crushed tomatoes, herbs, and ribs. Cover and place in the oven. Cook for 4 to 6 hours, or until the meat falls apart easily.

4. Remove from the oven and shred the meat with forks. Place the Dutch oven back on the stove and cook until the liquid is reduced by half. Set aside to cool and serve with the pasta of your choice.

*Nutritional Info: Calories: 326, Sodium: 1989 mg, Dietary Fiber: 7.7 g, Total Fat: 8.6 g, Total Carbs: 23.7 g, Protein: 23.3 g.*

# 10

## SEAFOOD DISHES

# Linguini with White Clam Sauce

*This classic shellfish dish is simple to make, and with fresh pasta from your Marcato pasta maker, you are sure to make a dish worthy of an Italian restaurant.*

*Servings: 6*
*Prep time: 20 minutes*
*Cook time: 30 minutes*

## Ingredients:

- 1 ball fresh egg pasta dough
- 4 tablespoons extra virgin olive oil
- 9 cloves garlic, smashed
- 60 littleneck clams
- 1 cup white wine
- 1/2 cup water
- 1 teaspoon red pepper flakes
- 2 tablespoons butter
- 2 tablespoons Italian parsley, chopped
- 2 tablespoons oregano, chopped
- Parmesan cheese for serving

## Directions:

1. Bring a large pot of water to a boil, and use your Marcato pasta maker to roll out your dough to the #5 setting. Then use the linguini cutting attachment to cut the sheets.

2. In a large skillet, heat half the oil and add half the garlic. Cook until the garlic is golden brown, then remove from the pan and discard. Add half the clams with the wine and water, and cook until the clams open. Remove the clams from the pan and reduce the cooking liquid. Remove the clams from their shells and pour the cooking liquid into a measuring cup.

3. Add the rest of the oil to the pan and add the remaining garlic. Cook until the garlic is golden brown, then discard the garlic. Add the

remaining clams and pepper flakes to the pan with the reserved cooking liquid. Cover and cook until the clams open.

4. Cook the linguini for 3 to 4 minutes, drain and add to the skillet. Chop the first batch of clams and add to the skillet. Stir everything and serve topped with parmesan cheese.

*Nutritional Info: Calories: 312, Sodium: 1147 mg, Dietary Fiber: 2.1 g, Total Fat: 14.5 g, Total Carbs: 36.9 g, Protein: 3.2 g.*

# Spaghetti with Shrimp and Tomato Sauce

*This zesty seafood pasta is an excellent way of using shrimp alongside pasta made fresh with your Marcato pasta maker.*

*Servings: 6*
*Prep time: 20 minutes*
*Cook time: 40 minutes*

## Ingredients:

*1 ball fresh egg pasta dough*

*2 tablespoons olive oil*

*3 cloves garlic, minced*

*4 cups tomatoes, diced*

*1 cup white wine*

*1 pound medium shrimp*

*2 tablespoons butter*

*1 teaspoon Cajun seasoning*

## Directions:

1. Bring a large pot of water to a boil, and use your Marcato pasta maker to roll out your dough to the #5 setting. Then use the spaghetti cutting attachment to cut the sheets.

2. In a large saucepan, heat half of the olive oil over medium heat. Add the garlic and cook until slightly softened. Add the tomatoes and wine, and simmer until the wine reduces by half. Then add the butter.

3. Cook the pasta for 2 to 3 minutes and drain.

4. Season the shrimp with Cajun seasoning. In another pan heat the rest of the olive oil and cook the shrimp until they are no longer translucent. Add the shrimp and pasta to the sauce and stir well before serving.

*Nutritional Info: Calories: 205, Sodium: 217 mg, Dietary Fiber: 1.5 g, Total Fat: 9.7 g, Total Carbs: 6.8 g, Protein: 17.6 g.*

# Smoked Salmon Alfredo

*This creamy salmon pasta works well with wide noodles like fettuccini, but use whatever type of pasta you feel like making with your Marcato pasta maker.*

*Servings: 4*
*Prep time: 10 minutes*
*Cook time: 20 minutes*

## Ingredients:

*1/2 ball fresh egg pasta dough*

*1 package cream cheese*

*3/4 cup parmesan cheese, grated*

*1/2 cup butter*

*1/2 cup milk*

*1 teaspoon garlic powder*

*1/4 teaspoon dried basil*

*1 tomato, chopped*

*1 pound smoked salmon, broken into small pieces*

## Directions:

1. Bring a large pot of water to a boil, and use your Marcato pasta maker to roll out your dough to the #5 setting. Then use the fettuccini cutting attachment to cut the sheets.

2. In a large saucepan, combine the cream cheese, parmesan, butter, milk, garlic, and stir over low heat until everything is creamy, about 10 to 15 minutes.

3. Cook the pasta for 2 to 3 minutes and drain.

4. Add the tomatoes to the sauce and stir until they have softened.

5. Add the salmon and the pasta to the sauce and stir. Serve topped with grated parmesan.

*Nutritional Info: Calories: 443, Sodium: 2543 mg, Dietary Fiber: 0.3 g, Total Fat: 36.8 g, Total Carbs: 3.5 g, Protein: 25 g.*

# Linguini al Frutti di Mare

*This fun traditional seafood pasta has its roots on the shores of the Amalfi Coast and uses a variety of fresh shellfish.*

*Servings: 4*
*Prep time: 20 minutes*
*Cook time: 30 minutes*

## Ingredients:

*1/2 ball fresh egg pasta dough*

*1 tablespoon olive oil*

*2 cloves garlic, sliced*

*1 teaspoon red pepper flakes*

*1/2 cup white wine*

*12 Manila or littleneck clams*

*3/4 cup tomato puree*

*12 black mussels*

*8 large shrimp*

*4 large diver scallops*

*5 ounces fresh calamari, cut into small rings*

*Parmesan cheese for serving.*

## Directions:

1. Bring a large pot of water to a boil, and use your Marcato pasta maker to roll out your dough to the #5 setting. Then use the linguini cutting attachment to cut the sheets.

2. In a large saucepan, heat the oil and cook the garlic until softened. Add the red pepper flakes, wine, and clams. Cover and cook until the clams open.

3. Cook the pasta for 3 to 4 minutes and drain.

4. To the saucepan, add the tomatoes and the rest of the seafood. Season with salt and pepper and stir until the mussels have opened. Toss in the linguini and stir to coat. Serve topped with parmesan cheese.

*Nutritional Info: Calories: 329, Sodium: 588 mg, Dietary Fiber: 1.4 g, Total Fat: 7.8 g, Total Carbs: 21.7 g, Protein: 34.4 g.*

# Shrimp Scampi

*This flavorful shrimp pasta is a restaurant classic and can be paired with virtually any pasta made with your Marcato pasta maker.*

*Servings: 4*
*Prep time: 10 minutes*
*Cook time: 30 minutes*

## Ingredients:

- 1/2 ball fresh egg pasta dough
- 2 tablespoons olive oil
- 1 pound large shrimp
- 6 tablespoons butter
- 6 cloves garlic, minced
- 1/2 teaspoon red pepper flakes
- 1/4 cup fresh parsley, chopped
- 2 teaspoons lemon zest
- 1 tablespoon fresh lemon juice
- Salt and black pepper

## Directions:

1. Bring a large pot of water to a boil, and use your Marcato pasta maker to roll out your dough to the #5 setting. Then use your choice of cutting attachment to cut the sheets.

2. In a large saucepan, heat the oil over medium-high heat, add the shrimp and cook until they are no longer translucent. Transfer to a plate and cover.

3. Cook the pasta for 2 to 3 minutes, drain, and set aside.

4. Melt the butter in the same saucepan, and add the garlic and red pepper. Stir in the cooked shrimp, parsley, lemon zest, and juice, and season with salt and pepper. Add the pasta and stir to combine.

*Nutritional Info: Calories: 315, Sodium: 269 mg, Dietary Fiber: 0.4 g, Total Fat: 24.4 g, Total Carbs: 4.4 g, Protein: 22 g.*

# Pappardelle with Salmon and Peas in Pesto Cream

*This rich yet light pasta dish is perfect for pappardelle noodles made fresh with your Marcato pasta maker.*

*Servings: 4*

*Prep time: 10 minutes*

*Cook time: 20 minutes*

## Ingredients:

- *1/2 ball fresh egg pasta dough*
- *1 cup fresh or frozen peas*
- *1 tablespoon olive oil*
- *1 12-ounce salmon filet, skin removed*
- *3/4 cup heavy cream*
- *1 tablespoon cream cheese*
- *2 tablespoons garlic, minced*
- *1/4 cup fresh basil, finely chopped*
- *1 tablespoon lemon juice*
- *Salt and black pepper*

## Directions:

1. Bring a large pot of water to a boil, and use your Marcato pasta maker to roll out your dough to the #5 setting. Then use a large knife to cut the sheets into 1-inch wide strips.

2. In a large skillet, heat the olive oil over medium heat. Season the salmon with salt and pepper and cook for 5 minutes per side. Transfer to a plate and chop into flakes.

3. In another large pan, add the cream over medium heat and simmer until slightly thickened. Reduce heat to low and add the cream cheese, garlic, and basil.

4. Cook the pasta for 3 to 4 minutes, drain and add to the pan with the sauce. Toss in the salmon and stir well.

*Nutritional Info: Calories: 621, Sodium: 1247 mg, Dietary Fiber: 2.3 g, Total Fat: 33.9 g, Total Carbs: 8.1 g, Protein: 72.1 g.*

# Lobster and Gruyere Fettuccini

*This decadent and creamy pasta uses chunks of real lobster and smoky gruyere for a flavor profile that is truly unique.*

*Servings: 4*

*Prep time: 30 minutes*

*Cook time: 30 minutes*

## Ingredients:

- 1/2 ball fresh egg pasta dough
- 6 tablespoons butter
- 3 tablespoons sweet onion, finely minced
- 1/4 cup flour
- 2 1/2 cups whole milk
- 12 ounces uncooked lobster tail meat, chopped
- 1 tablespoon dry sherry
- 1 teaspoon lemon zest
- Salt and black pepper
- 1 cup gruyere cheese
- 1 cup white cheddar cheese

## Directions:

1. Bring a large pot of water to a boil, and use your Marcato pasta maker to roll out your dough to the #5 setting. Then use the fettuccini cutting attachment to cut the sheets.

2. In a large saucepan, melt 3 tablespoons of butter, and add the onion, cooking until softened.

3. In a bowl, combine the flour and 1/2 cup milk and stir. Add the flour mixture and remaining milk to the saucepan and bring to a simmer. Add the lobster, sherry, lemon zest, salt and pepper. Cook for 2 minutes and remove from heat.

4. Cook the pasta for 2 to 3 minutes, drain and add to the saucepan. Cook for several minutes, stirring constantly, until the sauce has thickened.

*Nutritional Info: Calories: 672, Sodium: 969 mg, Dietary Fiber: 0.9 g, Total Fat: 43.5 g, Total Carbs: 27.3 g, Protein: 23.1 g.*

# Shrimp and Brie Linguini

*This filling pasta dish combines shrimp with creamy brie for a perfectly satisfying dish for any occasion.*

*Servings: 4*
*Prep time: 10 minutes*
*Cook time: 20 minutes*

## Ingredients:

- 1/2 ball fresh egg pasta dough
- 8 ounces brie, rind removed and cubed
- 1/4 cup sun-dried tomatoes, chopped
- 2 tomatoes, chopped
- 1/3 cup pitted Kalamata olives, chopped
- 2 cloves garlic, minced
- 1 cup fresh basil, chopped
- 1/4 cup olive oil
- 1 pound shrimp
- Salt and black pepper
- Parmesan cheese for serving

## Directions:

1. Bring a large pot of water to a boil, and use your Marcato pasta maker to roll out your dough to the #5 setting. Then use the linguini cutting attachment to cut the sheets.

2. In a large bowl, combine the brie, sun-dried and fresh tomatoes, olives, garlic, basil, salt, pepper, and olive oil. Stir and let stand for 1 hour.

3. Cook the pasta for 3 to 4 minutes, drain and toss with the brie mixture. Stir until brie is melted, then serve immediately, topped with parmesan cheese.

*Nutritional Info: Calories: 465, Sodium: 754 mg, Dietary Fiber: 0.6 g, Total Fat: 31.8 g, Total Carbs: 5.2 g, Protein: 38.9 g.*

# Capellini with Bay Scallops

*This dish uses delicate angel hair pasta with tender bay scallops to create a dish that is easy to make and incredibly well balanced.*

*Servings: 4*

*Prep time: 15 minutes*

*Cook time: 20 minutes*

## Ingredients:

- 1/2 ball fresh egg pasta dough
- 1 tablespoon vegetable oil
- 1 pound bay scallops
- 2 tablespoons butter
- 3 cloves garlic, minced
- 2 teaspoons lemon zest
- 1/2 teaspoon red pepper flakes
- 1/3 cup dry sherry
- 1 cup heavy cream
- Juice from 1 lemon
- Salt and black pepper
- Parmesan cheese for serving

## Directions:

1. Bring a large pot of water to a boil, and use your Marcato pasta maker to roll out your dough to the #5 setting. Then use the capellini cutting attachment to cut the sheets.

2. Cook the pasta for 2 minutes and drain.

3. In a large skillet, heat the oil until nearly smoking. Add the scallops and cook for 60 seconds. Add butter and stir until the butter is melted. Stir in the garlic, red pepper flakes, and lemon zest. Stir in the sherry, and stir until the alcohol cooks off, about 1 minute. Add the cream and reduce heat to low. Season with salt and pepper, and lemon juice.

4. Add the pasta to the skillet and stir well to coat the pasta. Serve topped with parmesan cheese.

*Nutritional Info: Calories: 298, Sodium: 257 mg, Dietary Fiber: 0.2 g, Total Fat: 21.6 g, Total Carbs: 5.7 g, Protein: 20.4 g.*

# Spaghetti with Spicy Mussels

*This assertive seafood dish uses red pepper flakes and fresh mussels along with spaghetti made with your Marcato pasta maker.*

*Servings: 4*
*Prep time: 20 minutes*
*Cook time: 30 minutes*

## Ingredients:

- 1 ball fresh egg pasta dough
- 2 cups crushed tomatoes
- 3 cloves garlic, chopped
- 1 shallot, chopped
- 1/2 cup white wine
- 2 pounds black mussels
- 2 tablespoons olive oil
- 1/2 teaspoon red pepper flakes
- 2 teaspoons fresh thyme, chopped
- 1/4 cup fresh parsley, finely chopped

## Directions:

1. Bring a large pot of water to a boil, and use your Marcato pasta maker to roll out your dough to the #5 setting. Then use the spaghetti cutting attachment to cut the sheets.
2. In a large skillet, combine the garlic and shallot with white wine. Bring to a boil and add the mussels. Cover and cook until the mussels open. Transfer the mussels to a bowl. When cooled slightly, remove half of the mussels from their shells. Pour the cooking liquid into a measuring cup.
3. Add oil to the pan and cook the red pepper flakes, then add the tomatoes and thyme. Turn up the heat to high and add half of the cooking liquid.
4. Cool the pasta for 2 to 3 minutes, drain, and add to the saucepan. Add the mussels and desired amount of cooking liquid. Season with salt and pepper and serve topped with fresh parsley.

*Nutritional Info: Calories: 343, Sodium: 896 mg, Dietary Fiber: 4.4 g, Total Fat: 12.3 g, Total Carbs: 21.9 g, Protein: 30.6 g.*

# Linguini with Calamari and Fennel

*This delicious linguini combines delicate calamari with flavorful fennel for a light, refreshing pasta that is great for any occasion.*

*Servings: 4*
*Prep time: 15 minutes*
*Cook time: 30 minutes*

## Ingredients:

*1/2 ball fresh egg pasta dough*

*5 tablespoons olive oil*

*1 pound squid, sliced 1/4 inch thick*

*1 fennel bulb, sliced*

*2 cloves garlic, sliced*

*3/4 teaspoon red pepper flakes*

*1/2 lemon, thinly sliced*

*1/2 cup parsley, chopped*

*Salt and black pepper*

## Directions:

1. Bring a large pot of water to a boil, and use your Marcato pasta maker to roll out your dough to the #5 setting. Then use the linguini cutting attachment to cut the sheets.

2. In a large skillet, heat 2 tablespoons of olive oil over high heat, season the squid with salt and pepper, and cook until just cooked through. Transfer to a bowl.

3. Reduce heat to medium and add 2 more tablespoons of olive oil. Add the fennel with salt and pepper. Cook until golden brown, then add the garlic, pepper flakes, and half of the lemon slices. Cook until the garlic is soft.

4. Boil the pasta for 3 to 4 minutes, drain and add to the skillet with 1 cup of the pasta cooking liquid. Toss in the calamari and serve topped with parsley.

*Nutritional Info: Calories: 283, Sodium: 87 mg, Dietary Fiber: 2.4 g, Total Fat: 19.4 g, Total Carbs: 10 g, Protein: 18.9 g.*

# Spicy Tilapia Spaghetti

*This easy-to-make dish is a healthy way to incorporate into your diet fresh fish and pasta made with your Marcato pasta maker.*

*Servings: 4*
*Prep time: 15 minutes*
*Cook time: 30 minutes*

## Ingredients:

*1/2 ball fresh egg pasta dough*

*2 tablespoons olive oil*

*2 cloves garlic, sliced*

*1/4 teaspoon cayenne pepper*

*1/2 teaspoon red pepper flakes*

*1 28-ounce can crushed tomatoes*

*1/2 teaspoon dried oregano*

*12 ounces fresh tilapia, cut into 3/4 inch pieces*

*10 Kalamata olives, quartered*

*1/2 cup parsley, chopped*

## Directions:

1. Bring a large pot of water to a boil, and use your Marcato pasta maker to roll out your dough to the #5 setting. Then use the spaghetti cutting attachment to cut the sheets.

2. In a large skillet over medium heat, add the garlic, 3/4 teaspoon salt, and pepper flakes. When the pan sizzles, add the tomatoes and oregano. Simmer 12 to 15 minutes.

3. Cook the pasta for 2 to 3 minutes, drain, and reserve 1 cup of the cooking water.

4. Add the fish and olives to the skillet, then add the pasta and the reserved cooking liquid. Simmer until the sauce has thickened and the fish is cooked through. Serve topped with chopped parsley.

*Nutritional Info: Calories: 233, Sodium: 515 mg, Dietary Fiber: 7.2 g, Total Fat: 9.2 g, Total Carbs: 18.7 g, Protein: 21.2 g.*

# Linguini with Red Clam Sauce

*This flavorful New York favorite is a take on the classic linguini with clam sauce that is full of flavor and depth.*

*Servings: 6*
*Prep time: 25 minutes*
*Cook time: 25 minutes*

## Ingredients:

- 1 ball fresh egg pasta dough
- 3 tablespoons olive oil
- 1 cup onion, diced
- 2 tablespoons garlic, minced
- 1 teaspoon red pepper flakes
- 1 cup dry white wine
- 1/4 cup tomato paste
- 1 28-ounce can crushed tomatoes
- 4 pounds littleneck clams
- 3 tablespoons fresh parsley, chopped
- 1/4 cup extra virgin olive oil

## Directions:

1. Bring a large pot of water to a boil, and use your Marcato pasta maker to roll out your dough to the #5 setting. Then use the linguini cutting attachment to cut the sheets.

2. In a large skillet, heat 3 tablespoons of olive oil over medium heat. Add the onions and cook until lightly caramelized. Add the garlic and pepper flakes, stir well and add the wine and tomato paste. Stir to combine, then add the crushed tomatoes, salt and black pepper.

3. Cook the pasta for 3 to 4 minutes, drain, and set aside.

4. Add the clams to the skillet and cook until the shells open. Add the parsley and toss in the pasta. Drizzle in the rest of the olive oil, stir, and serve.

*Nutritional Info: Calories: 399, Sodium: 1368 mg, Dietary Fiber: 6.5 g, Total Fat: 17.2 g, Total Carbs: 21 g, Protein: 6.2 g.*

# *Fideua*

*This traditional Spanish dish is basically paella with noodles instead of rice. Your Marcato makes perfect tasty pasta that will shine in this intricate dish.*

*Servings: 2*
*Prep time: 30 minutes*
*Cook time: 20 minutes*

## Ingredients:

*1/2 ball fresh egg pasta dough*

*1/2 cup olive oil*

*1/2 pound fresh squid, chopped into 1-inch pieces*

*10 large shrimp*

*2 cloves garlic, minced*

*1/4 cup Spanish onion, chopped*

*1 large tomato, chopped*

*Pinch of saffron*

*1/2 teaspoon smoked paprika*

*1/2 teaspoon bouillon cube*

*Salt and black pepper*

## Directions:

1. Bring a large pot of water to a boil, and use your Marcato pasta maker to roll out your dough to the #5 setting. Then use the capellini cutting attachment to cut the sheets. Then cut the capellini into 1-inch pieces.

2. In a large skillet, heat 3 tablespoons of olive oil over medium heat and add the uncooked pasta. Stir until it turns golden brown and remove from pan.

3. Add the rest of the oil to the pan, increase heat to high, and add the squid with some salt. When the squid is slightly browned, add the shrimp, garlic, and onion, and cook for 5 minutes.

4. Add the chopped tomato, saffron, and paprika and stir constantly for 2 minutes.

5. Add the bouillon and 2 cups of water. Bring to a boil and allow to simmer for 10 minutes. Then add the pasta. Cook until the water has been absorbed. Remove from heat, allow to rest for 3 minutes and serve.

*Nutritional Info: Calories: 602, Sodium: 133 mg, Dietary Fiber: 1.7 g, Total Fat: 52.8 g, Total Carbs: 11 g, Protein: 25.4 g.*

# Seafood Arrabbiata

*This mixed seafood dish is bold and flavorful while still allowing the delicate flavor of your fresh pasta to shine.*

*Servings: 4*
*Prep time: 20 minutes*
*Cook time: 15 minutes*

## Ingredients:

- 1 ball fresh egg pasta dough
- 2 tablespoons olive oil
- 6 ounces bay scallops
- 6 ounces medium shrimp
- 1/2 cup onion, chopped
- 1/2 teaspoon red pepper flakes
- 3 cloves garlic, minced
- 2 tablespoons tomato paste
- 1 medium tomato, diced
- 1/2 cup clam juice
- 12 littleneck clams
- 12 mussels
- 1 tablespoon fresh basil, chopped

## Directions:

1. Bring a large pot of water to a boil, and use your Marcato pasta maker to roll out your dough to the #5 setting. Then use the fettuccini cutting attachment to cut the sheets.

2. In a large skillet, heat 1 tablespoon olive oil over medium heat. Add the scallops and shrimp, cooking until no longer translucent. Transfer to a plate.

3. Heat the remaining olive oil and cook the onion, pepper flakes, and garlic for 2 minutes. Add the clam juice and clams. Reduce heat and cook until clams open. Then add the mussels. Stir in the scallop mixture and basil.

4. Cook the pasta for 3 to 4 minutes, drain, and add to the skillet. Stir to coat, and serve.

*Nutritional Info: Calories: 240, Sodium: 440 mg, Dietary Fiber: 1.3 g, Total Fat: 9.5 g, Total Carbs: 12.6 g, Protein: 26.7 g.*

# Shrimp Carbonara

*The combination of sautéed shrimp and crispy bacon goes perfectly with any pasta you choose to make with your Marcato pasta maker.*

*Servings: 4*
*Prep time: 15 minutes*
*Cook time: 20 minutes*

## Ingredients:

- 1 ball fresh egg pasta dough
- 2 large eggs
- 2 egg yolks
- 1 1/2 cup parmesan, grated
- 8 ounces bacon, cut into small pieces
- 1 pound medium shrimp
- 1/4 cup parsley, chopped

## Directions:

1. Bring a large pot of water to a boil, and use your Marcato pasta maker to roll out your dough to the #5 setting. Then use your choice of cutting attachment to cut the sheets.
2. In a bowl, combine the eggs, yolk, and parmesan.
3. In a large skillet over medium heat, cook the bacon until crisp. Transfer bacon to the bowl.
4. Cook the pasta and reserve 1/4 cup pasta cooking liquid. Add the liquid to the pan and add shrimp. Cook for 3 to 5 minutes.
5. Add the pasta to the skillet with the bacon mixture and toss to coat. Serve topped with chopped parsley.

*Nutritional Info: Calories: 485, Sodium: 1614 mg, Dietary Fiber: 0.1 g, Total Fat: 30 g, Total Carbs: 2.4 g, Protein: 50.2 g.*

# Spaghetti with Salmon and Leeks

*This flavorful, buttery pasta dish features the delicate flavor of fresh salmon and earthy leeks for a perfectly balanced dish you can make in no time.*

*Servings: 4*
*Prep time: 10 minutes*
*Cook time: 15 minutes*

## Ingredients:

- 1 ball fresh pasta dough
- 1 pound skinless salmon fillet
- 4 tablespoons butter
- 2 leeks, sliced
- 1/2 cup white wine
- Salt and black pepper

## Directions:

1. Bring a large pot of water to a boil, and use your Marcato pasta maker to roll out your dough to the #5 setting. Then use the spaghetti cutting attachment to cut the sheets.

2. Season the salmon with salt and pepper. In a large skillet, heat 2 tablespoons of butter over medium-high heat and cook the salmon 4 to 6 minutes per side and remove from pan. Add the leeks to the skillet and cook until they have softened. Then add the wine and reduce by half.

3. Boil the spaghetti for 2 to 3 minutes, drain, and add to the skillet. Chop the salmon into small pieced and toss with the pasta with the remaining butter.

*Nutritional Info: Calories: 379, Sodium: 163 mg, Dietary Fiber: 0.8 g, Total Fat: 24 g, Total Carbs: 11.5 g, Protein: 24.4 g.*

# Fettuccini with Crab, Cherry Tomatoes, and Basil

*This simple pasta dish highlights lump crab meat for a fresh yet decadent dish that will have your guests begging for more.*

*Servings: 4*
*Prep time: 15 minutes*
*Cook time: 20 minutes*

## Ingredients:

- 1 ball fresh pasta dough
- 1 tablespoon olive oil
- 2 cloves garlic, chopped
- 1/2 teaspoon red pepper flakes
- 1 cup cherry tomatoes, quartered
- Zest and juice from 1 lemon
- 3/4 pound fresh crab meat
- 2 teaspoons capers
- 1 cup fresh basil, chopped

## Directions:

1. Bring a large pot of water to a boil, and use your Marcato pasta maker to roll out your dough to the #5 setting. Then use the fettuccini cutting attachment to cut the sheets.

2. In a large skillet over medium-high heat, add the oil, garlic, and pepper flakes. Cook until the garlic is golden, then add the tomatoes and cook until they start to break down. Add the lemon juice and remove from heat. Stir in the crab.

3. Boil the pasta for 3 to 4 minutes, drain, and add to the skillet. Add the lemon zest, capers, and basil.

*Nutritional Info: Calories: 145, Sodium: 579 mg, Dietary Fiber: 0.8 g, Total Fat: 5.4 g, Total Carbs: 9.6 g, Protein: 12.3 g.*

# Creamy Lobster Linguini

*This rich, decadent treat is a perfect way to highlight the wholesome flavor of your fresh, homemade pasta.*

*Servings: 6*
*Prep time: 20 minutes*
*Cook time: 40 minutes*

## Ingredients:

*1 ball fresh pasta dough*

*3 tablespoons olive oil*

*2 slices bacon, chopped*

*3 shallots, minced*

*2 cloves garlic, minced*

*1/4 teaspoon red pepper flakes*

*2 cups tomato puree*

*1/4 cup heavy cream*

*1/2 cup parmesan, grated*

*1/2 cup basil, chopped*

*1 1/2-pound steamed lobster*

## Directions:

1. Bring a large pot of water to a boil, and use your Marcato pasta maker to roll out your dough to the #5 setting. Then use the linguini cutting attachment to cut the sheets.

2. In a large saucepan, heat olive oil over medium heat. Add the bacon and cook until crisp. Add the shallots, garlic, and pepper flakes and cook until fragrant. Add the tomato puree and cream. Reduce heat to low and simmer for 5 minutes

3. Boil the pasta for 3 to 4 minutes, drain, and add to the saucepan. Add the parmesan and lobster and stir well. Serve topped with parmesan cheese.

*Nutritional Info: Calories: 232, Sodium: 580 mg, Dietary Fiber: 1.7 g, Total Fat: 10.2 g, Total Carbs: 11.8 g, Protein: 24 g.*

# *Capellini with Oysters*

*This rich dish highlights fresh oysters and delicate angel hair pasta for a flavorful and memorable meal.*

*Servings: 6*
*Prep time: 15 minutes*
*Cook time: 25 minutes*

## Ingredients:

- 1 ball fresh pasta dough
- 3 tablespoons olive oil
- 1 cup green onion, sliced
- 1/2 cup parsley, chopped
- 3 cloves garlic, chopped
- 4 cups oysters, drained
- 2 tablespoons lemon juice
- Salt and black pepper
- 1/2 cup parmesan cheese

## Directions:

1. Bring a large pot of water to a boil, and use your Marcato pasta maker to roll out your dough to the #5 setting. Then use the capellini cutting attachment to cut the sheets.

2. In a large saucepan, heat the oil and add the onion, parsley, and garlic, stirring until tender. Add the oyster, reduce heat, and cook for 5 minutes. Stir in the lemon juice, salt and pepper.

3. Boil the pasta for 2 minutes, drain, and add to the saucepan. Add the cheese and stir well.

*Nutritional Info: Calories: 115, Sodium: 57 mg, Dietary Fiber: 0.7 g, Total Fat: 8.2 g, Total Carbs: 6.6 g, Protein: 4.5 g.*

# 11

---

## FILLED PASTA DISHES

# Ricotta Ravioli

*This traditional ravioli is simple and delicious. Fresh pasta from your Marcato pasta maker will make this dish really come alive.*

*Servings: 4*
*Prep time: 20 minutes*
*Cook time: 10 minutes*

## Ingredients:

- 1 ball fresh pasta dough
- 1 12-ounce container ricotta cheese
- 1/2 cup parmesan cheese, finely grated
- 3 tablespoons parsley, finely chopped
- 1 egg, beaten

## Directions:

1. Bring a large pot of water to a boil, and use your Marcato pasta maker to roll out your dough to the #7 setting.

2. In a bowl, combine the ricotta, parmesan, and parsley. Stir well.

3. Lay the pasta sheets out on a table and spoon 1 tablespoon balls of ricotta mixture 2 inches apart. Use a brush to brush a small amount of egg along the edges of the sheets and in between the ricotta.

4. Fold the sheets over and press the edges and the space between the ricotta. Try to remove as much air as possible. Use a knife or ravioli cutter to separate the raviolis. Boil for 5 to 6 minutes, drain, and serve with your favorite sauce.

*Nutritional Info: Calories: 237, Sodium: 291 mg, Dietary Fiber: 0.6 g, Total Fat: 11.6 g, Total Carbs: 17.9 g, Protein: 15.4 g.*

# Ravioli with Sage Walnut Butter

*This delightfully nutty, savory sauce is perfectly paired with your homemade ricotta ravioli.*

*Servings: 4*
*Prep time: 10 minutes*
*Cook time: 15 minutes*

## Ingredients:

*1/4 cup balsamic vinegar*

*2 teaspoons honey*

*1 bay leaf*

*1 batch homemade ricotta ravioli*

*6 tablespoons butter*

*1/3 cup fresh sage leaves*

*1 cup walnuts*

*3/4 cup parmesan cheese, grated*

## Directions:

1. In a medium saucepan, combine the vinegar, honey, and bay leaf over medium heat. Cook until syrupy.

2. Cook the ravioli for 5 to 6 minutes and drain.

3. In a large skillet, melt the butter and add the sage and walnuts. Cook about 3 minutes, then add 1 cup of the pasta cooking water. Boil and reduce by half.

4. Add the ravioli to the skillet and stir, then add the vinegar mixture. Serve topped with parmesan cheese.

*Nutritional Info: Calories: 417, Sodium: 236 mg, Dietary Fiber: 3.3 g, Total Fat: 38.9 g, Total Carbs: 9 g, Protein: 12.6 g.*

# Crab Ravioli with Tomato Cream

*This delicious seafood ravioli is enhanced with a delicate and silky tomato cream and homemade pasta.*

*Servings: 4*
*Prep time: 30 minutes*
*Cook time: 20 minutes*

## Ingredients:

- 1 ball fresh pasta dough
- 6 ounces lump crab meat
- 1/2 cup ricotta cheese
- 1 egg, beaten
- 1 cup milk
- 1 28-ounce can crushed tomatoes
- 2 tablespoons butter
- 1 tablespoon fresh basil, chopped

## Directions:

1. Bring a large pot of water to a boil, and use your Marcato pasta maker to roll out your dough to the #7 setting.

2. In a bowl, combine the crab meat, and ricotta. Spoon 1 tablespoon-sized balls onto the pasta sheets. Brush with egg and fold over. Cut into individual raviolis.

3. In a large saucepan, combine the milk, butter, crushed tomatoes, and milk. Simmer over medium heat until smooth.

4. Boil the raviolis for 5 to 6 minutes, drain, and add the pan with the sauce. Stir to coat, and serve.

*Nutritional Info: Calories: 270, Sodium: 771 mg, Dietary Fiber: 6.5 g, Total Fat: 24.5 g, Total Carbs: 24.5 g, Protein: 18.4 g.*

# Fig and Gorgonzola Ravioli

*This decadent fried ravioli is great as an appetizer or a savory dessert.*

*Servings: 6*
*Prep time: 20 minutes*
*Cook time: 30 minutes*

## Ingredients:

*1 ball fresh pasta dough*

*1/2 cup vegetable oil*

*3 tablespoons butter*

*1-1/2 cups apple cider*

*1 cinnamon stick*

*10 figs, halved*

*1/2 cup gorgonzola*

*1/4 cup toasted walnuts, chopped*

*1 egg, beaten*

## Directions:

1. Bring a large pot of water to a boil, and use your Marcato pasta maker to roll out your dough to the #7 setting.

2. In a medium saucepan, melt the butter and cook until it smells nutty. Add the apple cider and cinnamon and bring to a boil. Cook about 20 minutes, strain and set aside.

3. Lay out your pasta sheets and place fig halves about 2 inches apart and add some crumbles of gorgonzola around each fig. Brush the edges with egg and fold over. Cut into individual raviolis.

4. In a large skillet, heat the oil over medium heat and add the raviolis. Cook until crispy and place on paper towels. Drizzle with the cider reduction and serve.

*Nutritional Info: Calories: 415, Sodium: 251 mg, Dietary Fiber: 4 g, Total Fat: 32.5 g, Total Carbs: 28.7 g, Protein: 6.7 g.*

# Three Cheese Tortellini

*This fun, filled pasta is easier to make than it looks, and your freshly made pasta dough will give it real homemade character.*

*Servings: 6*
*Prep time: 20 minutes*
*Cook time: 30 minutes*

## Ingredients:

- *1 ball fresh pasta dough*
- *1 cup ricotta cheese*
- *1/2 cup parmesan cheese*
- *1/2 cup asiago cheese*
- *1/4 cup parsley, chopped*
- *1/2 teaspoon salt*

## Directions:

1. Bring a large pot of water to a boil, and use your Marcato pasta maker to roll out your dough to the #6 setting.
2. In a large bowl, combine the cheeses, parsley, and salt. Stir well.
3. Use a 3-inch round cookie cutter to make round pieces of pasta dough. Place a teaspoon of filling in the middle of each piece of dough. Fold the dough over, join the corners, and press together.
4. Boil the tortellini for 5 to 6 minutes, drain and serve with your favorite sauce.

*Nutritional Info: Calories: 87, Sodium: 308 mg, Dietary Fiber: 0.2 g, Total Fat: 4.7 g, Total Carbs: 4.6 g, Protein: 6.6 g.*

# Beef and Pork Filled Tortellini

*This flavorful, filled pasta is perfect for any meal and pairs well with a wide variety of sauces.*

*Servings: 6*
*Prep time: 30 minutes*
*Cook time: 30 minutes*

## Ingredients:

*1 ball fresh pasta dough*

*1 tablespoon butter*

*1/4 pound ground beef*

*1/4 pound ground pork*

*2 tablespoons white wine*

*2 ounces prosciutto, sliced*

*1 egg, beaten*

*1/4 cup parmesan cheese, grated*

*Salt and black pepper*

## Directions:

1. Bring a large pot of water to a boil, and use your Marcato pasta maker to roll out your dough to the #6 setting.

2. In a large saucepan, melt the butter and add the beef and pork. Cook for 10 minutes, then add the wine and cook for another 10 minutes.

3. In a food processor, combine the beef and pork mixture with the prosciutto and pulse several times. Pour the mixture into a large bowl and add the egg, cheese, and a dash of salt and pepper.

4. Use a 3-inch cookie cutter to make rounds with the pasta dough. Spoon 1 teaspoon of meat into the center of each round, fold over, and join the corners, pressing to seal.

5. Boil the tortellini for 5 to 6 minutes, drain and serve.

*Nutritional Info: Calories: 161, Sodium: 231 mg, Dietary Fiber: 0.3 g, Total Fat: 6.6 g, Total Carbs: 9 g, Protein: 15 g.*

# *Mushroom Tortellini*

*This rustic tortellini filling uses different types of mushrooms to create an earthy, rich flavor that is sure to impress the entire family.*

*Servings: 6*
*Prep time: 45 minutes*
*Cook time: 45 minutes*

## Ingredients:

- *1 ball fresh pasta dough*
- *5 ounces shiitake mushrooms, minced*
- *5 ounces cremini mushrooms, minced*
- *5 ounces oyster mushrooms, minced*
- *3 tablespoons butter*
- *2 shallots, minced*
- *3 cloves garlic, minced*
- *1 teaspoon thyme, minced*
- *1/2 cup red wine*
- *Salt and black pepper*
- *1/2 cup parmesan cheese, grated*

## Directions:

1. Bring a large pot of water to a boil, and use your Marcato pasta maker to roll out your dough to the #6 setting.

2. In a large skillet over medium heat, melt the butter and add all of the mushrooms and cook until soft, about 3 to 5 minutes. Add the shallots, garlic, and thyme, and season with salt and pepper. Reduce heat and cook until all of the liquid has cooked off.

3. Add the wine and cook until wine has cooked off. Mix in the parmesan and transfer to a food processor. Blend until smooth.

4. Use a 3-inch round cutter to cut the pasta. Place 1 teaspoon of the mushroom filling into the middle of each pasta round, fold over, and pinch together the corners.

5. Cook the tortellini for 4 to 5 minutes, drain, and serve drizzled with olive oil.

*Nutritional Info: Calories: 204, Sodium: 178 mg, Dietary Fiber: 3.4 g, Total Fat: 7.2 g, Total Carbs: 21.8 g, Protein: 9.8 g.*

# Butternut Squash Ravioli

*This comforting fall favorite is savory and a little sweet for a well-balanced and slightly nutty flavor that is sure to be a hit with your guests.*

*Servings: 6*
*Prep time: 30 minutes*
*Cook time: 90 minutes*

## Ingredients:

- 1 ball fresh egg pasta dough
- 2 pounds butternut squash, peeled and cubed
- 6 cloves garlic, peeled
- 10 fresh sage leaves
- 2/3 cup roasted pine nuts
- 1 cup parmesan cheese
- Olive oil
- Salt and black pepper

## Directions:

1. Bring a large pot of water to a boil, and use your Marcato pasta maker to roll out your dough to the #6 setting.

2. Heat oven to 400°F and place squash on a large baking sheet. Drizzle with olive oil and season with salt and pepper. Roast for 45 to 50 minutes. Add the sage leaves to the pan when 10 minutes remain.

3. In a food processor, combine the squash, 1/3 cup pine nuts, and 1/2 cup parmesan and blend to a thick paste.

4. Spoon 1 tablespoon of the filling onto the pasta sheets 2 inches apart and fold the pasta over. Then use a knife or ravioli cutter to cut individual raviolis.

5. Boil the raviolis for 5 to 6 minutes, drain, and serve drizzled with olive oil and topped with the remaining parmesan.

*Nutritional Info: Calories: 268, Sodium: 183 mg, Dietary Fiber: 5 g, Total Fat: 17.3 g, Total Carbs: 23.9 g, Protein: 10.3 g.*

# Sausage Ravioli

*This hearty meat-filled ravioli is full of robust flavors, but the star of the show is always the fresh pasta from your Marcato pasta maker.*

*Servings: 6*
*Prep time: 20 minutes*
*Cook time: 30 minutes*

## Ingredients:

*1 ball fresh egg pasta dough*

*3/4 pound sweet Italian sausage, casings removed*

*2 eggs, beaten*

*2 tablespoons parmesan cheese*

*2 tablespoons shallot, minced*

*2 tablespoons olive oil*

## Directions:

1. Bring a large pot of water to a boil, and use your Marcato pasta maker to roll out your dough to the #6 setting.

2. In a large skillet, heat the oil over high heat and brown the sausage and remove from the pan.

3. In a large bowl, combine the sausage, eggs, shallot, and parmesan. Mix well.

4. Place 1 tablespoon of the sausage filling onto the pasta sheets 2 inches apart. Fold the sheets over and use a knife or ravioli cutter to separate the raviolis. Boil for 5 to 6 minutes, drain, and serve drizzled with olive oil or with your favorite tomato sauce.

*Nutritional Info: Calories: 157, Sodium: 357 mg, Dietary Fiber: 0.1 g, Total Fat: 11.2 g, Total Carbs: 3.1 g, Protein: 11.4 g.*

# Chicken and Spinach Ravioli

*This healthy and delicious chicken ravioli is perfect when paired with freshly made pasta from your Marcato pasta maker.*

*Servings: 6*
*Prep time: 30 minutes*
*Cook time: 30 minutes*

## Ingredients:

*1 ball fresh pasta dough*

*1 cup cooked ground chicken*

*8 ounces spinach, chopped*

*3 tablespoons butter, melted*

*3 tablespoons parmesan cheese*

*Salt and black pepper*

## Directions:

1. Bring a large pot of water to a boil, and use your Marcato pasta maker to roll out your dough to the #6 setting.

2. In a large bowl, combine the chicken, spinach, and butter. Stir well, then add the cheese, salt, and pepper.

3. Place 1 tablespoon of filling onto the pasta sheets 2 inches apart. Fold the sheets over, and use a knife or ravioli cutter to separate the raviolis.

4. Boil the raviolis for 5 to 6 minutes, drain, and serve topped with olive oil and parmesan cheese.

*Nutritional Info: Calories: 119, Sodium: 113 mg, Dietary Fiber: 0.9 g, Total Fat: 8.1 g, Total Carbs: 3.6 g, Protein: 8.4 g.*

# Bolognese Ravioli with Fresh Tomato Sauce

*This rich and hearty ravioli is perfect for a winter night thanks to a flavor profile that is complex and comforting.*

*Servings: 6*
*Prep time: 60 minutes*
*Cook time: 30 minutes*

## Ingredients:

1 ball fresh egg pasta dough

2 tablespoons butter

1 small onion, chopped

1/2 cup carrot, shredded

1/2 cup celery, finely chopped

3/4 pound ground beef

1/2 cup red wine

2 eggs, beaten

1/2 cup parmesan cheese, grated

1/4 cup bread crumbs

1/4 cup olive oil

4 cloves garlic

1 28-ounce can crushed tomatoes

Salt and black pepper

## Directions:

1. Bring a large pot of water to a boil, and use your Marcato pasta maker to roll out your dough to the #6 setting.

2. In a large skillet over medium heat, melt the butter and add the onion, carrot, and celery, cooking until slightly browned. Add the beef, salt, and pepper, and cook until the meat is browned. Add the wine and simmer until the wine has cooked off. Remove from heat and allow to cool.

3. In a food processor, add the beef, eggs, 1/2 cup cheese, and breadcrumbs. Pulse until blended.

4. In a large saucepan over medium heat, add the oil and garlic and simmer until golden. Add the tomatoes and simmer until slightly reduced.

5. Place 1 tablespoon of filling 2 inches apart on the pasta sheets, fold the pasta over, and use a knife or ravioli cutter to separate the raviolis. Boil the raviolis for 5 to 6 minutes, drain, and top with tomato sauce.

*Nutritional Info: Calories: 346, Sodium: 405 mg, Dietary Fiber: 5.2 g, Total Fat: 17.9 g, Total Carbs: 19.6 g, Protein: 23.6 g.*

# Creamy Four-Cheese Ravioli

*This rich and creamy blend of cheeses works in perfect harmony with freshly made pasta from your Marcato pasta maker and pairs perfectly with your favorite sauce.*

*Servings: 6*
*Prep time: 20 minutes*
*Cook time: 20 minutes*

## Ingredients:

- 1 ball fresh pasta dough
- 8 ounces ricotta cheese
- 4 ounces cream cheese, softened
- 1/2 cup mozzarella cheese, shredded
- 1/2 cup provolone cheese, shredded
- 1 egg
- 2 teaspoons dried parsley

## Directions:

1. Bring a large pot of water to a boil, and use your Marcato pasta maker to roll out your dough to the #6 setting.
2. In a large bowl, combine the cheeses, egg and parsley, and mix well.
3. Place 1 tablespoon of filling onto the sheets, brush the edges with egg, and fold over. Use a knife or ravioli cutter to separate the raviolis.
4. Boil the raviolis for 5 to 6 minutes, drain, and serve with your favorite sauce.

*Nutritional Info: Calories: 187, Sodium: 241 mg, Dietary Fiber: 0.1 g, Total Fat: 14 g, Total Carbs: 5 g, Protein: 10.5 g.*

# Pumpkin Ravioli

*This amazing fall ravioli is perfect for entertaining any night of the week. The delicate pumpkin flavor pairs perfectly with your freshly made pasta.*

*Servings: 4*
*Prep time: 40 minutes*
*Cook time: 60 minutes*

## Ingredients:

*1 ball fresh egg pasta dough*

*8 tablespoons butter*

*1 pound pumpkin, peeled and cubed*

*2 cups heavy cream*

*2 tablespoons fresh sage, minced*

*2 teaspoons fresh thyme, minced*

*3 eggs, beaten*

*2 cups chicken broth*

*2 shallots, minced*

## Directions:

1. Bring a large pot of water to a boil, and use your Marcato pasta maker to roll out your dough to the #6 setting.

2. In a large skillet over medium heat, melt 4 tablespoons butter. When the butter foams, add the pumpkin and cook until soft.

3. Transfer the pumpkin to a large pan and add half of the cream and half of the herbs. Cook for 30 minutes, or until the liquid has cooked off. Remove from heat and add 2 more tablespoons of butter. Stir in 2 of the eggs and season with salt and pepper.

4. Place 1 tablespoon of filling 2 inches apart on the pasta sheets, and brush the edges of the sheets with egg. Fold the sheets over and use a knife or ravioli cutter to separate the raviolis.

5. Boil the raviolis for 5 to 6 minutes, drain, and serve drizzled with olive oil or melted butter.

*Nutritional Info: Calories: 545, Sodium: 646 mg, Dietary Fiber: 4 g, Total Fat: 50.3 g, Total Carbs: 16.6 g, Protein: 10.1 g.*

# 12

## BAKED PASTAS

# Baked Four-Cheese Spaghetti

*This rich and decadent baked spaghetti is a deeply flavorful way to get the most out of pasta hand crafted with the Marcato pasta maker.*

*Servings: 8*
*Prep time: 20 minutes*
*Cook time: 60 minutes*

## Ingredients:

- 1 ball fresh pasta dough
- 1/2 pound fontina, shredded
- 1/2 pound mozzarella, shredded
- 1/2 pound gruyere, shredded
- 1/4 pound gorgonzola, crumbled
- Salt and black pepper

## Directions:

1. Bring a large pot of water to a boil, and use your Marcato pasta maker to roll out your dough to the #5 setting, and use the spaghetti attachment to cut the sheets.
2. Preheat oven to 350°F, and butter a 9-by-13-inch baking dish.
3. Boil spaghetti for 2 to 3 minutes and drain.
4. In a large bowl, combine the fontina, mozzarella, and gruyere. Place 1/3 of the pasta in the baking dish and sprinkle on 1/3 of the cheese mix and 1/2 of the gorgonzola. Repeat until all the pasta and cheese has been used.
5. Bake until the top is golden brown, about 40 minutes.

*Nutritional Info: Calories: 291, Sodium: 523 mg, Dietary Fiber: 0.5 g, Total Fat: 22.6 g, Total Carbs: 3.1 g, Protein: 19.8 g.*

# *Classic Meat Lasagna*

*This baked Italian classic is hearty and comforting, and thanks to freshly made pasta sheets, it is packed with flavor.*

*Servings: 8*
*Prep time: 30 minutes*
*Cook time: 60 minutes*

## Ingredients:

*1 ball fresh pasta dough*

*1 pound ground beef*

*1/2 pound sweet Italian sausage*

*1/2 pound hot Italian sausage*

*2 cloves garlic, chopped*

*1 teaspoon dried oregano*

*12 ounces ricotta cheese*

*Salt and black pepper*

*1 cup parmesan cheese, grated*

*1 28-ounce can crushed tomatoes*

*2 cups mozzarella, shredded*

## Directions:

1. Bring a large pot of water to a boil, and use your Marcato pasta maker to roll out your dough to the #5 setting. Trim the sheets into even rectangles. Preheat oven to 350°F.

2. In a large skillet over high heat, brown the beef and sausage and set aside.

3. In a Dutch oven, combine the meat, tomatoes, garlic, oregano, salt and pepper. Simmer for 15 minutes.

4. Boil the pasta sheets for 3 to 4 minutes and drain.

5. Grease a large baking dish and pour a small amount of sauce into the bottom. Spread the sauce evenly, then add a layer of pasta sheets. On top of the pasta, add a layer of cheese, then repeat until you have run

out of sauce, pasta, and cheese. Cover with foil and bake for 30 minutes. Remove the foil and bake an additional 10 to 15 minutes.

*Nutritional Info: Calories: 419, Sodium: 840 mg, Dietary Fiber: 3.3 g, Total Fat: 21.9 g, Total Carbs: 31.5 g, Protein: 41.3 g.*

# Roasted Butternut Squash Lasagna

*This light yet flavorful take on lasagna uses sweet and savory squash for a flavor that is perfect for a brisk fall day.*

*Servings: 8*
*Prep time: 60 minutes*
*Cook time: 60 minutes*

## Ingredients:

- 1 ball fresh pasta dough
- 1 butternut squash, peeled and seeded
- 3 tablespoons olive oil
- 1/4 cup chicken or vegetable broth
- 1 teaspoon ground nutmeg
- 1 teaspoon fresh sage, minced
- 3/4 cup parmesan, grated
- 1/4 cup butter
- 1/4 cup flour
- 2 1/4 cups milk
- Salt and black pepper
- 1-1/2 cups mozzarella, shredded

## Directions:

1. Bring a large pot of water to a boil, and use your Marcato pasta maker to roll out your dough to the #6 setting. Cut the dough into even rectangles. Preheat oven to 400°F.

2. Place squash on a baking sheet and drizzle with olive oil and season with salt and pepper. Bake for 25 to 30 minutes, or until tender.

3. In a food processor, combine the squash, nutmeg, sage, and cheese. Blend until smooth.

4. In a medium saucepan, combine the butter, flour, milk, and salt and bring to a light boil, let thicken, and remove from heat.

5. Boil the pasta sheets and drain. Grease a large baking dish and pour in a small amount of sauce, then alternate noodles, cheese and sauce until all are used. Cover with foil and bake at 375°F for 30 minutes, then remove foil and bake an additional 10 to 15 minutes.

*Nutritional Info: Calories:210 , Sodium: 210 mg, Dietary Fiber: 0.5 g, Total Fat: 15.9 g, Total Carbs: 9.5 g, Protein: 8.9 g.*

# Baked Manicotti

*This classic dish is full of cheesy goodness, and best of all it is very easy to make.*

*Servings: 4*
*Prep time: 20 minutes*
*Cook time: 60 minutes*

## Ingredients:

*1 ball fresh pasta dough*

*1 pint ricotta*

*8 ounces mozzarella, shredded*

*3/4 cup parmesan*

*2 eggs*

*1 28-ounce can crushed tomatoes*

*1 teaspoon dried oregano*

*1 teaspoon dried basil*

*Salt and black pepper*

## Directions:

1. Bring a large pot of water to a boil, and use your Marcato pasta maker to roll out your dough to the #6 setting. Cut sheets into even squares. Preheat oven to 350°F.

2. In a large pot, combine the tomatoes, oregano, and basil. Simmer for 10 to 15 minutes and remove from heat. Season with salt and pepper.

3. In a large bowl, combine the ricotta, mozzarella, 1/2 cup parmesan, eggs, salt and pepper.

4. Pour sauce into a large baking dish so that it evenly coats the bottom.

5. Boil the pasta and then spoon cheese mixture onto each one. Roll the pasta squares over so that they form tubes and place them in the baking dish. Cover with sauce and top with parmesan cheese. Bake for 45 minutes.

*Nutritional Info: Calories: 531, Sodium: 1128 mg, Dietary Fiber: 6.7 g, Total Fat: 27.1 g, Total Carbs: 28.7 g, Protein: 45 g.*

# Baked Spaghetti Marinara

*This easy-to-make baked spaghetti dish makes a perfect family meal, and best of all, it couldn't be easier to make.*

*Servings: 8*
*Prep time: 30 minutes*
*Cook time: 60 minutes*

## Ingredients:

- 1 ball fresh pasta dough
- 1 pound ground beef
- 1 onion, chopped
- 1 28-ounce can crushed tomatoes
- 3 cloves garlic, minced
- 1 tablespoon fresh basil, chopped
- 2 eggs
- 1/3 cup parmesan, grated
- 5 tablespoons butter, melted
- 2 cups cottage cheese
- 4 cups mozzarella, shredded

## Directions:

1. Bring a large pot of water to a boil, and use your Marcato pasta maker to roll out your dough to the #5 setting. Use the spaghetti attachment to cut the sheets. Preheat oven to 350°F.

2. In a large skillet over medium heat, cook the beef and onion until the beef is browned.

3. Boil the spaghetti, drain, and add to the skillet. Add the tomatoes, garlic, and herbs.

4. In a large bowl, combine the eggs, parmesan, and butter. Add to the skillet.

5. Grease a large baking dish and add half of the spaghetti mixture, then top with half of the cottage cheese, meat sauce, and mozzarella. Repeat until you have run out of ingredients.

6. Cover with foil and bake for 40 minutes. Uncover and bake another 20 minutes or until cheese is melted.

*Nutritional Info: Calories: 361, Sodium: 704 mg, Dietary Fiber: 3.6 g, Total Fat: 17.6 g, Total Carbs: 14.2 g, Protein: 36.1 g.*

# Roasted Vegetable and Ravioli Lasagna

*This brilliant combination of classic ravioli with lasagna is the perfect way to use your freshly made cheese raviolis.*

*Servings: 4*
*Prep time: 15 minutes*
*Cook time: 60 minutes*

## Ingredients:

- 1 pound sweet Italian sausage, casings removed
- 1 28-ounce can crushed tomatoes
- 2 tablespoons fresh basil, chopped
- 1/2 cup water
- 24 homemade cheese raviolis
- 12 ounces mozzarella, shredded
- 3 tablespoons parmesan, grated
- 1 1/2 pounds mixed roasted vegetables, cut into small pieces
- 2 tablespoons olive oil

## Directions:

1. Preheat oven to 375°F. Boil a large pot of water and cook the raviolis for 5 to 6 minutes.

2. In a large saucepan, heat the oil and brown the sausage. Then add the tomatoes and basil. Simmer for 10 minutes. Cook the raviolis and drain. Add the vegetables to the sauce.

3. Grease a large baking dish and layer the raviolis, vegetables, and mozzarella. Top with parmesan and cover with foil. Bake for 30 minutes, remove foil and continue baking for another 20 minutes.

*Nutritional Info: Calories: 668, Sodium: 1638 mg, Dietary Fiber: 13.9 g, Total Fat: 32.3 g, Total Carbs: 44.3 g, Protein: 52.6 g.*

# *Pumpkin Lasagna*

*This take on classic lasagna is perfect for entertaining in the fall.*

*Servings: 4*
*Prep time: 30 minutes*
*Cook time: 60 minutes*

## Ingredients:

*1 ball fresh pasta dough*

*2 tablespoons olive oil*

*1 onion, chopped*

*1/2 teaspoon ground nutmeg*

*3 cups pumpkin puree*

*1-1/2 cups heavy cream*

*1-1/2 cups parmesan cheese, grated*

*1/2 cup milk*

*Salt and black pepper*

## Directions:

1. Bring a large pot of water to a boil, and use your Marcato pasta maker to roll out your dough to the #6 setting. Cut the sheets into even rectangles. Preheat oven to 400°F.

2. In a large skillet, heat the oil over medium heat and add the onions, stirring until translucent. Season with salt and pepper.

3. In a bowl, combine 2 cups of pumpkin, 3/4 cup cream, 1/2 cup parmesan, 1/4 teaspoon nutmeg, and season with salt and pepper.

4. Boil the pasta for 3 to 4 minutes and drain.

5. Pour the milk into an 8-by-12-inch baking dish. Top the milk with 1/3 of the pasta sheets, 1/2 the pumpkin mix and another layer of noodles. Repeat until all ingredients are used. Cover with foil and bake for 20 minutes. Uncover and bake an additional 15 minutes.

*Nutritional Info: Calories: 319, Sodium: 192 mg, Dietary Fiber: 6.1 g, Total Fat: 22.9 g, Total Carbs:23.7 g, Protein: 9 g.*

# Baked Tagliatelle with Chicken

*This fun take on a classic chicken bake is made even more unique with the addition of freshly made tagliatelle from your Marcato pasta maker.*

*Servings: 4*
*Prep time: 20 minutes*
*Cook time: 40 minutes*

## Ingredients:

- 1 ball fresh pasta dough
- 1 onion, sliced
- 1 tablespoon vegetable oil
- 12 ounces chicken breast, cut into slices
- 1 can cream of chicken soup
- 2 tablespoons whole grain mustard
- 1 red bell pepper, chopped
- 8 ounces broccoli, chopped

## Directions:

1. Bring a large pot of water to a boil, and use your Marcato pasta maker to roll out your dough to the #5 setting. Use a knife to cut sheets into 1-inch-wide strips. Preheat oven to 450°F.
2. In a medium saucepan, heat the oil and cook the onion until translucent.
3. Add the chicken, pepper and broccoli and cook an additional 5 minutes. Add the soup and mustard to the pan and stir until thick.
4. Boil the pasta for 3 to 4 minutes, drain and place in a greased baking dish. Pour the sauce on top and bake for 20 minutes.
5. Serve with garnish of choice.

*Nutritional Info: Calories: 260, Sodium: 623 mg, Dietary Fiber: 2.6 g, Total Fat: 11 g, Total Carbs: 17.8 g, Protein: 22.5 g.*

# *Fettuccini Al Forno*

*This old fashioned, cheesy baked fettuccini is easy to make and is sure to delight the entire family.*

*Servings: 4*
*Prep time: 25 minutes*
*Cook time: 40 minutes*

## Directions:

*1 ball fresh pasta dough*

*4 tablespoons olive oil*

*1 eggplant, cubed*

*10 sun-dried tomatoes, chopped*

*15 black olives, pitted and chopped*

*2 cloves garlic, chopped*

*2 cups tomato puree*

*1 1/2 cups mozzarella, shredded*

*1/2 cup smoked gruyere, shredded*

## Directions:

1. Bring a large pot of water to a boil, and use your Marcato pasta maker to roll out your dough to the #5 setting and use the fettuccini attachment to cut the sheets.

2. In a large saucepan, heat the oil and add the eggplant, sun-dried tomatoes, olives, and garlic. Cook for several minutes, then add the tomato puree. Let simmer for 10 minutes.

3. Boil the pasta, drain, and add to the pan. Stir well and place half into a greased baking dish, then top with half of the mozzarella and gruyere. Add the rest of the pasta and cheese. Bake for 25 to 30 minutes.

*Nutritional Info: Calories: 378, Sodium: 331 mg, Dietary Fiber: 10.8 g, Total Fat: 23.7 g, Total Carbs: 35.1 g, Protein: 13.7 g.*

# Baked Pasta Primavera

*This healthy vegetable pasta bake is a perfect way to get the entire family excited about eating delicious, fresh veggies.*

*Serving: 6*
*Prep time: 30 minutes*
*Cook time: 60 minutes*

## Ingredients:

- *1 ball fresh pasta dough*
- *1 cup shredded carrots*
- *1 cup fresh peas*
- *1 cup sliced zucchini*
- *1 cup asparagus, cut into small pieces*
- *2 tablespoons butter*
- *2 tablespoons flour*
- *1 cup milk*
- *1/2 cup chicken broth*
- *1/2 cup feta cheese*
- *1/2 cup diced tomatoes*
- *1/2 cup parmesan*
- *Salt and black pepper*

## Directions:

1. Bring a large pot of water to a boil, and use your Marcato pasta maker to roll out your dough to the #5 setting. Use the spaghetti attachment to cut the sheets.

2. Pre-heat oven to 400°F and line a baking dish with foil.

3. In a saucepan, melt the butter and whisk in the flour and salt. Sauté the vegetables for 10 minutes, then add the tomatoes and chicken broth. Remove from heat.

4. Boil the pasta for 2 to 3 minutes, drain, and add to the saucepan. Stir in the feta and transfer to the baking dish. Pour in the milk, stir, and

add 1/2 of the parmesan. Bake for 20 minutes and top with the remaining parmesan.

*Nutritional Info: Calories: 166, Sodium: 327 mg, Dietary Fiber: 2,7 g, Total Fat: 9 g, Total Carbs: 14.3 g, Protein: 8 g.*

# Cheesy Baked Tortellini

*This easy recipe uses tortellini you have made fresh with your Marcato pasta maker.*

*Servings: 6*
*Prep time: 10 minutes*
*Cook time: 35 minutes*

## Ingredients:

- 1 pound fresh tortellini
- 2 cups marinara sauce
- 1/3 cup mascarpone
- 1/4 cup parsley, chopped
- 2 teaspoons fresh thyme, chopped
- 1/3 cup smoked mozzarella, sliced
- 1/4 cup parmesan, grated

## Directions:

1. Preheat oven to 350°F and oil an 8-by-8 baking dish.
2. In a large bowl, combine the tomato sauce, mascarpone, parsley and thyme. Stir together and add the uncooked tortellini. Stir well.
3. Pour the pasta mixture into the baking dish, top with mozzarella and parmesan, and bake for 30 minutes, or until golden brown.

*Nutritional Info: Calories: 400, Sodium: 726 mg, Dietary Fiber: 5.2 g, Total Fat: 11.5 g, Total Carbs: 45.2 g, Protein: 16 g.*

# Baked Chicken Cannelloni

*This delicious, rich cannelloni dish uses the freshest ingredients, including fresh pasta, for the best tasting, healthiest cannelloni ever.*

*Servings: 6*
*Prep time: 20 minutes*
*Cook time: 35 minutes*

## Ingredients:

- 1 ball fresh pasta dough
- 4 cups cooked chicken breast, finely chopped
- 1 10-ounce package frozen spinach, chopped
- 10 ounces cream cheese
- 1 cup ricotta
- 1 cup mozzarella, shredded
- 1/2 cup breadcrumbs
- 1 teaspoon garlic powder
- Salt and black pepper

## Directions:

1. Bring a large pot of water to a boil and use your Marcato pasta maker to roll out your dough to the #6 setting. Cut the sheets into squares. Preheat oven to 350°F.

2. In a large bowl, combine the cheeses, chicken, spinach, breadcrumbs, garlic powder, salt and pepper. Mix well.

3. Boil the pasta sheets, drain, and spoon 4 tablespoons of filling into the center of each. Roll the sheets into tubes.

4. Grease a large baking dish and arrange the cannelloni side by side. Bake for 25 to 30 minutes.

*Nutritional Info: Calories: 637, Sodium: 493 mg, Dietary Fiber: 1.6 g, Total Fat: 29.1 g, Total Carbs: 14.3 g, Protein: 75.9 g.*

# 13

## ASIAN PASTA DISHES

# Chicken Chow Mein

*This recipe for classic chicken chow mein will have you recreating your favorite Chinese restaurant dishes at home in no time!*

*Servings: 4*
*Prep time: 25 minutes*
*Cook time: 10 minutes*

## Ingredients:

*1 ball fresh egg pasta dough*

*1/2 pound chicken thighs, cut into small pieces*

*2 tablespoons vegetable oil*

*3 cups cabbage, shredded*

*1 carrot, shredded*

*1 cup bean sprouts*

*2 cloves garlic, minced*

*1/4 cup water*

*2 teaspoons cornstarch*

*2 tablespoons soy sauce*

*2 tablespoons oyster sauce*

*2 tablespoons Chinese cooking wine*

## Directions:

1. Bring a large pot of water to a boil and use your Marcato pasta maker to roll out your dough to the #5 setting. Use the spaghetti attachment to cut the sheets. Boil the pasta and drain.

2. In a large pan or wok, heat the oil over high heat and add the garlic. Cook until fragrant and add the chicken, cooking until no longer pink. Remove from pan. Discard garlic.

3. In the pan, combine the soy sauce, oyster sauce, wine, and water. Then stir in the vegetables and chicken. Add the noodles last and cook, stirring constantly for several minutes.

*Nutritional Info: Calories: 243, Sodium: 699mg, Dietary Fiber: 1.9 g, Total Fat: 11.9 g, Total Carbs: 13.7 g, Protein:20.3 g.*

# Classic Pad Thai

*This flavorful Thai dish is actually quite easy to make at home, and thanks to fresh rice noodles made with your Marcato, you will be sure to have an authentic-tasting dish.*

*Servings: 6*
*Prep time: 40 minutes*
*Cook time: 20 minutes*

## Ingredients:

- 1 ball rice noodle dough
- 2 tablespoons butter
- 1 pound chicken breasts, cut into small pieces
- 1/4 cup vegetable oil
- 4 eggs
- 1 tablespoon white wine vinegar
- 2 tablespoons fish sauce
- 3 tablespoons sugar
- 1/4 tablespoon red pepper flakes
- 2 cups bean sprouts
- 1/4 cup crushed peanuts

## Directions:

1. Bring a large pot of water to a boil, and use your Marcato pasta maker to roll out your dough to the #5 setting. Use the spaghetti cutting attachment to cut the sheets.

2. In a large skillet, heat the butter over medium heat and cook the chicken until browned. Remove from pan and set aside.

3. Crack the eggs into the hot oil and cook until firm. Then stir in the chicken and cook for 5 minutes. Then add the noodles, vinegar, fish sauce, sugar, and red pepper. Mix well, and add bean sprout. Cook another 3 minutes and serve.

*Nutritional Info: Calories: 354, Sodium: 611 mg, Dietary Fiber: 0.2g, Total Fat: 22.4 g, Total Carbs: 10 g, Protein: 28.9 g.*

# Spicy Cold Peanut Noodles

*These spicy noodles are great on their own or as a side dish for grilled chicken or shrimp.*

*Servings: 8*
*Prep time: 15 minutes*
*Cook time: 15 minutes*

## Ingredients:

- *1 ball fresh egg pasta dough*
- *1/3 cup creamy peanut butter*
- *3 tablespoons sesame oil*
- *1/2 teaspoon red pepper flakes*
- *1/4 teaspoon cayenne pepper*
- *2 green onions, thinly sliced*
- *2 tablespoons toasted sesame seeds*
- *2 tablespoons soy sauce*

## Directions:

1. Bring a large pot of water to a boil, and use your Marcato pasta maker to roll out your dough to the #5 setting. Use the spaghetti attachment to cut the sheets. Boil the pasta for 2 to 3 minutes and drain.
2. In a large bowl, combine the rest of the ingredients. Add the pasta to the bowl and stir well to coat the pasta. Place in the refrigerator and serve when cold.

*Nutritional Info: Calories: 135 , Sodium: 289 mg, Dietary Fiber: 1.2 g, Total Fat: 12 g, Total Carbs: 5 g, Protein: 3.7 g.*

# Beef Noodle Stir Fry

*This flavorful Asian dish doesn't take long to make, but its complex flavors are sure to delight the entire family.*

*Servings: 6*
*Prep time: 20 minutes*
*Cook time: 20 minutes*

## Ingredients:

- 1 ball fresh egg pasta dough
- 1 tablespoon olive oil
- 8 ounces top sirloin, thinly sliced
- 1 cup cremini mushrooms, sliced
- 1 cup broccoli, chopped
- 2 carrots, sliced
- 1/3 cup soy sauce
- 3 tablespoons oyster sauce
- 1 tablespoon brown sugar
- 1 tablespoon ginger, grated
- 2 cloves garlic, minced
- 1 teaspoon sesame oil

## Directions:

1. Bring a large pot of water to a boil, and use your Marcato pasta maker to roll out your dough to the #5 setting. Use the spaghetti attachment to cut the sheets.
2. In a bowl, whisk together the soy sauce, brown sugar, garlic, sesame oil, and ginger.
3. In a large skillet, heat the oil over high heat and cook the beef until browned. Remove from pan.
4. Boil the pasta for 2 to 3 minutes, and drain.

5. Add the mushrooms, broccoli, and carrots to the skillet and cook until tender. Stir in the noodles and soy sauce mixture. Cook for 3 to 4 minutes and serve.

*Nutritional Info: Calories: 294 , Sodium: 995 mg, Dietary Fiber: 1.3 g, Total Fat: 11.2 g, Total Carbs:9.4 g, Protein: 37.6 g.*

# Sesame Noodles

*These classic staple noodles are easy to make and taste great hot or cold!*

*Servings: 6*
*Prep time: 10 minutes*
*Cook time: 15 minutes*

## Ingredients:

- 1 ball fresh egg pasta dough
- 1/4 cup soy sauce
- 2 tablespoons sugar
- 4 cloves garlic
- 2 tablespoons rice vinegar
- 3 tablespoons sesame oil
- 1/2 teaspoon hot chili oil
- 4 tablespoons vegetable oil
- 4 green onions, sliced

## Directions:

1. Bring a large pot of water to a boil, and use your Marcato pasta maker to roll out your dough to the #5 setting. Use the spaghetti cutting attachment to cut the sheets.
2. In a large bowl, combine everything except the noodles and onions.
3. Boil pasta for 2 to 3 minutes and drain.
4. Add the noodles to the sauce and stir well. Add the green onions and serve.

*Nutritional Info: Calories: 194, Sodium: 618 mg, Dietary Fiber: 0.5 g, Total Fat: 17.5 g, Total Carbs: 8.4 g, Protein: 1.3 g.*

# *Pad See Ew*

*This Thai classic uses fresh rice noodles for a flavorful and healthy stir fry that everyone will love.*

*Servings: 4*
*Prep time: 15 minutes*
*Cook time: 15 minutes*

## Ingredients:

- *1 ball rice noodle dough*
- *2 tablespoons soy sauce*
- *2 tablespoons oyster sauce*
- *2 teaspoons white vinegar*
- *2 teaspoons sugar*
- *2 teaspoons water*
- *2 tablespoons vegetable oil*
- *2 cloves garlic, smashed*
- *4 cups Chinese broccoli*

## Directions:

1. Bring a large pot of water to a boil, and use your Marcato pasta maker to roll out your dough to the #6 setting. Use the fettuccini attachment to cut the sheets.

2. In a large skillet, heat the oil over medium heat and brown the garlic. Add the rest of the ingredients and sauté for 10 minutes or until the broccoli has softened slightly. You can also toss in some chopped chicken or pork and brown until cooked through.

*Nutritional Info: Calories: 107, Sodium: 514 mg, Dietary Fiber: 2.4 g, Total Fat: 7.5 g, Total Carbs: 9.4 g, Protein: 1.7 g.*

# Shrimp Lo Mein

*This classic dish is rich in flavor, and thanks to pasta made fresh with your Marcato, it will taste as authentic as possible.*

*Servings: 6*
*Prep time: 20 minutes*
*Cook time: 15 minutes*

## Ingredients:

- 1 ball fresh egg pasta dough
- 1 pound shrimp
- 1/4 cup soy sauce
- 3 tablespoons oyster sauce
- 1 tablespoon mirin
- 1 cup cremini mushrooms, sliced
- 2 cups cabbage, shredded
- 1 onion, sliced
- 2 cloves garlic, minced
- 3 tablespoons vegetable oil

## Directions:

1. Bring a large pot of water to a boil, and use your Marcato pasta maker to roll out your dough to the #5 setting. Use the spaghetti attachment to cut the sheets. Boil the pasta for 2 to 3 minutes and drain.

2. In a large skillet, heat the oil over high heat and add the garlic and onion. Cook until browned, then add the mushrooms, cabbage, soy sauce, oyster sauce, and mirin. Cook until the mushrooms are soft, then add the shrimp. Cook until the shrimp is pink, then add the noodles and cook another 5 minutes.

*Nutritional Info: Calories: 192, Sodium: 883 mg, Dietary Fiber: 1.2 g, Total Fat: 8.5 g, Total Carbs: 9.4 g, Protein: 19.1 g.*

# Miso Noodles

*This fusion recipe uses fresh egg noodles from your Marcato as well as savory miso paste for deep, rich flavors.*

*Servings: 6*
*Prep time: 20 minutes*
*Cook time: 15 minutes*

## Ingredients:

- *1 ball fresh egg pasta dough*
- *1 tablespoon vegetable oil*
- *3 tablespoons white miso paste*
- *2 teaspoons ginger, grated*
- *1 clove garlic, minced*
- *1 tablespoon soy sauce*
- *3 tablespoons water*
- *2 green onions, sliced*
- *Sesame seeds for topping*

## Directions:

1. Bring a large pot of water to a boil, and use your Marcato pasta maker to roll out your dough to the #5 setting. Use the spaghetti attachment to cut the sheets. Boil the pasta for 2 to 3 minutes and drain.

2. In a large skillet, heat the oil over medium heat. Add the garlic and ginger and cook for 3 minutes, stirring constantly. Add the soy sauce, water, and miso paste. Stir well then add the pasta. Serve topped with green onion and sesame seeds.

*Nutritional Info: Calories: 60, Sodium: 344 mg, Dietary Fiber: 0.5 g, Total Fat: 3.5 g, Total Carbs: 5.4 g, Protein: 1.8 g.*

# Shiitake and Scallion Noodles

*This dish gets its distinct flavor from earthy Shiitake mushrooms and noodles made fresh with your Marcato pasta maker.*

*Servings: 6*
*Prep time: 20 minutes*
*Cook time: 15 minutes*

## Ingredients:

- 1 ball fresh egg pasta dough
- 1/4 pound snow peas
- 1/4 cup soy sauce
- 1/4 cup mirin
- 2 teaspoons toasted sesame oil
- 3 tablespoons vegetable oil
- 1 pound Shiitake mushrooms, sliced
- 6 scallions, sliced
- 1 tablespoon ginger, grated
- 2 tablespoons water
- 2 tablespoons chopped cilantro

## Directions:

1. Bring a large pot of water to a boil, and use your Marcato pasta maker to roll out your dough to the #5 setting. Use the spaghetti attachment to cut the sheets. Boil the pasta for 2 to 3 minutes and drain.

2. In a large skillet, heat the oil over medium heat and cook the peas for 2 minutes. Add the mushrooms and cook until browned. Add the scallions and ginger, then add the water and sesame oil.

3. Add the noodles and soy sauce and cook for another 4 to 5 minutes. Serve topped with cilantro.

*Nutritional Info: Calories: 166, Sodium: 888 mg, Dietary Fiber: 2.8 g, Total Fat: 9 g, Total Carbs: 21.2 g, Protein: 3.2 g.*

# Ramen Salad with Peanuts

*This fresh ramen noodle salad makes a perfect lunch on a warm day. It can be served hot or cold.*

*Servings: 4*
*Prep time: 10 minutes*
*Cook time: 10 minutes*

## Ingredients:

- 1 ball fresh egg pasta dough
- 1/2 cup peanut butter
- 1/4 cup water
- 1/4 cup vinegar
- 1/4 cup teriyaki sauce
- 1/2 teaspoon garlic, minced
- 1/2 teaspoon red pepper flakes
- 1 cucumber, sliced
- 1 carrot, shredded
- 2 green onions, thinly sliced
- 1/2 cup peanuts, crushed

## Directions:

1. Bring a large pot of water to a boil, and use your Marcato pasta maker to roll out your dough to the #5 setting. Use the spaghetti attachment to cut the sheets. Boil the pasta for 2 to 3 minutes and drain.

2. In a large bowl, stir together the peanut butter, water, vinegar, teriyaki, garlic, and red pepper. Toss in the noodles and stir well. Add the cucumber, carrots, peanuts, and green onions, and serve.

*Nutritional Info: Calories: 353, Sodium: 882 mg, Dietary Fiber: 4.6 g, Total Fat: 25.9 g, Total Carbs: 20.5 g, Protein: 15.2 g.*

# Red Curry Noodles

*This spicy, rich dish is the perfect way to showcase rice noodles made fresh with your Marcato pasta maker.*

*Servings: 6*
*Prep time: 20 minutes*
*Cook time: 15 minutes*

## Ingredients:

- *1 ball fresh rice noodle dough*
- *2 tablespoons vegetable oil*
- *4 tablespoons red curry paste*
- *1 tablespoon garlic, minced*
- *1 can coconut milk*
- *1 pound medium shrimp*
- *1 red bell pepper, sliced*
- *Salt and black pepper*

## Directions:

1. Bring a large pot of water to a boil, and use your Marcato pasta maker to roll out your dough to the #5 setting. Use the spaghetti attachment to cut the sheets. Boil the pasta for 2 to 3 minutes and drain.

2. In a large saucepan, heat the oil over high heat and cook the shrimp until pink. Remove from pan.

3. Add the coconut milk, curry paste, garlic, red pepper and salt and pepper. Simmer for 5 to 6 minutes. Add the shrimp and noodles and stir well.

*Nutritional Info: Calories: 261 , Sodium: 699 mg, Dietary Fiber: 1.3 g, Total Fat: 18 g, Total Carbs: 8 g, Protein: 17.5 g.*

# Pancit

*This Filipino favorite is easy to make and packs lots of flavors. It's a perfect way to use freshly made rice noodles.*

*Servings: 6*
*Prep time: 10 minutes*
*Cook time: 15 minutes*

## Ingredients:

- *1 ball fresh rice noodle dough*
- *1 teaspoon vegetable oil*
- *1 onion, diced*
- *3 cloves garlic, minced*
- *2 cups cooked chicken breast, chopped*
- *1/4 cup soy sauce*
- *1 head cabbage, sliced*
- *4 carrots, sliced*

## Directions:

1. Bring a large pot of water to a boil, and use your Marcato pasta maker to roll out your dough to the #5 setting. Use the capellini attachment to cut the sheets. Boil the pasta for 2 to 3 minutes and drain.

2. In a large skillet, heat the oil and then cook the onion and garlic until soft. Add the chicken, cabbage, carrots, and soy sauce. Toss in the noodles and cook until everything is heated.

*Nutritional Info: Calories: 247 , Sodium: 727 mg, Dietary Fiber: 4.6 g, Total Fat: 4.7 g, Total Carbs: 15.8 g, Protein: 34.6 g.*

# Shanghai Noodles

*This spicy noodle dish has lots of intense flavor, but it still allows your homemade noodles to shine.*

*Servings: 6*
*Prep time: 20 minutes*
*Cook time: 20 minutes*

## Ingredients:

- 1 ball fresh egg pasta dough
- 2 tablespoons vegetable oil
- 1/4 cup soy sauce
- 1 tablespoon red chili paste
- 2 tablespoons sesame oil
- 2 green onions, chopped
- 1 pound ground pork
- 2 cups shredded cabbage
- 1 cup bean sprouts

## Directions:

1. Bring a large pot of water to a boil, and use your Marcato pasta maker to roll out your dough to the #5 setting. Use the spaghetti attachment to cut the sheets. Boil the pasta for 2 to 3 minutes and drain.

2. In a large skillet over high heat, add the oil and cook the ground pork until no longer pink. Add the soy sauce, chili paste, cabbage, and sprouts. Cook 3 to 4 minutes and stir well. Add the noodles and sesame oil, and serve topped with green onions.

*Nutritional Info: Calories: 232, Sodium: 696 mg, Dietary Fiber: 0.9 g, Total Fat: 12.7 g, Total Carbs: 7 g, Protein: 22.6 g.*

# Taiwanese Beef Noodle Soup

*This classic Taiwanese dish is full of complex flavors and is a warm, comforting meal on a cold winter night.*

*Servings: 6*
*Prep time: 20 minutes*
*Cook time: 2 hours*

## Ingredients:

*1 ball fresh rice noodle dough*

*2-1/2 pound boneless beef short rib, cut into chunks*

*8 cups water*

*1/2 cup soy sauce*

*1/4 cup Chinese cooking wine*

*1 tablespoon sugar*

*3 cloves garlic, chopped*

*2 star anise pods*

*1 teaspoon toasted sesame oil*

## Directions:

1. Bring a large pot of water to a boil, and use your Marcato pasta maker to roll out your dough to the #5 setting. Use the spaghetti attachment to cut the sheets. Boil the pasta for 2 to 3 minutes and drain.

2. In a large pot or Dutch oven, combine the short ribs, water, soy sauce, garlic, wine, sugar, and star anise, and bring to a boil. Let simmer for 2 hours.

3. Strain the broth through a mesh strainer and return to the pot. Add the sesame oil.

4. Place some noodles in a bowl and pour in broth and add several pieces of beef.

*Nutritional Info: Calories: 320, Sodium: 1317 mg, Dietary Fiber: 17.4 g, Total Fat: 10.3 g, Total Carbs: 6.4 g, Protein: 47.5 g.*

# What's better than a free cookbook?

# 20 FREE COOKBOOKS!

**Finally, a way to get all of the cookbooks you've wanted, for completely free!**

HHF Press has published over 100 cookbooks since 2014, and due to new technology we can now give you 20 of our most popular cookbooks for absolutely free!

You'll receive the same well written, professionally designed cookbooks we sell on Amazon, Barnes & Noble and other retailers.

**Here are some of the cookbooks included:**
Electric Pressure Cooker, Perfect Outdoor Grill, Dutch Oven, Sous Vide, Air Fryer, and many more...

**Get them today! No purchase necessary.**

## Go to: www.HHFPress.com/20/pasta

Printed in Great Britain
by Amazon